Families
under the
Influence

Families under the Influence

Changing Alcoholic Patterns

Michael Elkin

W·W·NORTON & COMPANY

New York   *London*

The text of this book is composed in Times Roman, with display type set
in Times Roman. Composition and manufacturing by The Maple-Vail
Book Manufacturing Group.
Book design by Jacques Chazaud.

First Edition

Library of Congress Cataloging in Publication Data

Elkin, Michael.
Families under the influence.

Includes index.
1. Alcoholism.   2. Alcoholics—Family relationships.
3. Family psychotherapy.   I. Title.
RC565.E44   1984   616.86'1   83–21933

ISBN 0-393-01770-2

W. W. Norton & Company, Inc.
500 Fifth Avenue New York, N.Y. 10110
W. W. Norton & Company Ltd.
37 Great Russell Street London WC1B 3NU

1   2   3   4   5   6   7   8   9   0

For my mother and father

CONTENTS

AUTHOR'S NOTE

S uccessful therapy, I believe, is an exchange of gifts in which therapist and client mutually and simultaneously teach each other and help each other grow. This book is an attempt to discharge the debt I feel to countless alcoholics and their families for their aid in my personal and professional growth.

Until fairly recently, traditional service delivery systems—hospitals, mental health clinics, and medical centers—were spectacularly ineffective with alcohol and drug abusers. As a result, the treatment of this clientele tended to be entrusted to alternative programs largely staffed by exabusers, aspiring professionals lacking the qualifications for employment at traditional facilities, and a few maverick professionals who sought a freedom to experiment that was not available at mainstream agencies.

Although I did not fall into the latter group, these alternative agencies allowed me and many others the opportunity to develop alternative approaches to treatment which are now increasingly accepted and utilized by the mainstream of service providers. It is my hope that this book will help to accelerate that process.

From 1970–1973 I worked for Project Place in Boston, doing

some counseling but mostly working as a "drug expert" advising towns, schools, and treatment facilities how best to deal with the "drug menace." At that time I had few effective suggestions, but my role gave me the chance to observe closely the state of the art of drug-abuse prevention and treatment.

From 1973–1975 I was clinical director of Atlantis, a small community drug-treatment facility in Stoneham, Massachusetts. Because I was then studying family therapy at the Boston Family Institute in Brookline, Massachusetts, I was extremely interested in meeting the families of the young drug abusers referred to us. Of the more than one hundred families in whose treatment I participated, nearly all turned out to have at least one person who suffered from alcoholism. Some of these parents were out of the home and some were recovering, but the correlation between teenage drug abuse and parental alcoholism was almost invariable.

From 1975–1981 I worked at the North Shore Council on Alcoholism in Danvers, Massachusetts, first as a family therapist and then as director of training. In this latter capacity I consulted with over sixty institutions—hospitals, mental health agencies, alcoholism and drug agencies, and schools. During this period I met with members of hundreds of alcoholic families, with many more presented to me for consultation. As can be expected, some generalizations emerged.

One of these was that alcoholism was a major factor in many cases in which the presenting symptom had little or nothing to do with drinking. Most of the clients were directly related to an alcoholic or were alcoholics themselves. In case after case school and behavior problems, depression, and psychotic symptoms could be linked to alcoholism in a family member. This is not to say that these other symptoms were "caused" by alcoholism, but it became increasingly clear that effective treatment of these symptoms was difficult if not impossible unless the drinking was addressed.

Contrary to my expectations, I began to note that the most difficult phase in the treatment of alcoholism is not the "drying out" phase in which the alcoholic is learning to cope with the loss of the drug, but the task of helping the alcoholic to realize that drinking is a problem in the first place. This job is made more difficult because people surrounding the alcoholic tend to collude in protecting the drinker from this realization. Incredibly, it seemed that family, friends, and colleagues would organize to support and facilitate the drinking which caused them so much misery and frustration. Seen individually, the actions of these people seemed "crazy," destructive, and inexplicable. Seen as a group, however, there was a logic in which this "crazy" behavior began to make sense. Thus, I began to see alcoholism not simply as a disease suffered by individuals, but also as a pattern performed by a system. It stood to reason that changing this pattern could make the individual more accessible to alcoholism treatment.

However, this is not a book about the *treatment* of alcoholism. Many successful models exist to aid alcoholics in their recovery once they acknowledge their condition. This book will attempt to orient clinicians toward alcoholic family systems so that intervention can facilitate the *beginning* of alcoholism treatment.

Alcoholics Anonymous is a brilliantly thought-out and extremely effective treatment program for alcoholics, but fewer than one-tenth of this nation's alcoholics enter the program. The remaining 90-odd percent have not yet "hit bottom," i.e., suffered so many tragic and destructive losses to themselves and others that they recognize the problem. This book will present strategies for working with alcoholic families so that the process of recovery can begin sooner—raising the "bottom" so that people experience less pain and tragedy before they accept treatment.

Before presenting treatment strategies, I will discuss the power dynamics of drunkenness and how it works in a system. I will describe a typical family with an alcoholic father, review some of the pitfalls in working with alcoholic clients, and present a model for intervention. The second part of the book is an attempt to convey the experience of treatment both unsuccessful and successful of a hypothetical alcoholic family.

At the time I was gathering data for this book, very few families with alcoholic mothers came into treatment. There may be two quite opposite reasons for this. One, it is far easier both economically and culturally for a husband to leave an alcoholic wife than for a wife to leave an alcoholic husband; as a result many alcoholic women come into treatment only after they have lost their families. Second, it is usually easier to shield a mother from the world. A family can surround the mother with a protective cushion while she quietly drinks herself to death.

In any case, because I lack sufficient data to generalize with confidence, there is little in this book about families with alcoholic mothers. Although the general treatment strategies described here are effective with these families as well, a detailed description of the workings of families with alcoholic mothers is a task which must be accomplished by someone else. I hope, however, that this book will be useful within the limits described.

There are many people who have provided help and support; only a few can be cited here. Julia O'Brian, the executive director of the North Shore Council on Alcoholism when I was there, gave me the time and technical support to complete the original manuscript. Thanks are due to Rochelle Ruthchild, Ph.D., for loving and helpful carrots and sticks, to Laurie Brown, Ed.D., for her sensitive editing of the original manuscript, and to Ann McGonagle for her transcriptions. I am grateful to Drs. Fred and Bunny Duhl for helping me realize that I had something to say, and to my therapist and friend, Dick Chasin, M.D., for helping me acquire the courage and discipline to say it.

For their love and forbearance, my wife, Rachel, and my sons, Max and Eli, deserve boundless credit. I thank Carol Green, a typist with a sense of humor, and special thanks go to Carol Houck Smith, my editor at Norton, whose skills, patience, and wisdom I will forever appreciate.

Michael Elkin

October, 1983

PART I

Power:
Who's in Charge
Here?

1

Why Do People Get Drunk? The Development of an Alcoholic System

In Western cultures the evaluation and treatment of aberrant behavior has long been entrusted to the field of medicine. In light of this it is not surprising that we have been taught to think of extremely eccentric or socially dysfunctional behavior the way a doctor thinks of illness: as a pathological invasion of a healthy system which produces undesirable systems and is attributable to a root cause either known or unknown.

Medical science as we know it matured with the discoveries popularly associated with Louis Pasteur. He was the first to see that much disease can be traced to external agents that produce symptoms seemingly unrelated to themselves. In other words, it was at first difficult to connect a patient's fever and pain with the minute beasts swimming in his bloodstream. Once this connection was made, physicians were on to the cosmic joke. They began to see that the body was a system in which an attack in one place could produce an effect in another. The symptom was a distraction in their search for a root cause.

Freud is the best-known translator of these concepts to the realm of behavior. With the exception of paresis and a few other conditions, the search for "microbs of madness" had not shown much progress. But when Freud saw that some forms of paralysis could be temporarily relieved through hypnosis, he realized that germs were not the only possible root cause of pathology. His discovery, which rivaled Pasteur's in importance and eclipsed it in intellectual elegance, viewed the psyche as a system that was at least as complex as the physical system. As in the physical system, the symptomatic expression of pathology may be related to the root cause in ways that seem obscure and indirect. Therefore, when Freud encountered a paralysis or a phobia, he was less concerned with those outward signs than he was in discovering why the patient developed the system. He looked at the germs, not the lesion.

In *The Family Crucible,* Carl Whitaker and Augustus Napier advance the hypothesis that Freud dismissed families as being the "root cause" of pathology after he found that his patients' tales of traumatic abuse were untrue. This setback, Napier surmises, led Freud to abandon the view that incidents and patterns of family life were central to the development of symptoms. Rather, he felt that symptoms were an expression of a relatively closed internal system. Freud did, however, note the effects of family life on the course of psychoanalysis. He refused to treat patients who were living with their families because he felt that the families interfered with the treatment.

This view of socially dysfunctional behavior or psychiatric symptoms ignores one of the most interesting and important features of these phenomena, the social and interpersonal patterns that surround them. The systems point of view is merely a shift to a larger systemic context: the social and interactional context rather than the intrapsychic context. Another way of saying this is that a systems-oriented therapist is much more interested in what a particular behavior does in the social system in which it occurs than in its intrapsychic origins.

The advantages for a therapist who takes this point of view are many: First, the therapist gets to deal with observable phenomena rather than abstract constructs. Second, it is easier to conceptualize and organize data about social behavior than about infinitely complex and abstract intrapsychic systems. Third, it is easier to design interventions which will be effective in changing patterns of social interaction. And fourth, it is easier to evaluate an intervention on a social system because the therapist is trying to effect observable events.

Regardless of the comparative validity of the two points of view, it is hard to deny that a therapist working from a systems point of view has an easier and more simply conceived task. It is also easier for him or her to get relatively reliable feedback about the work.

A Cambridge psychiatrist, John Pierce, once remarked that alcoholism is now the "popular" disease because it responds well to systems therapy, just as hysterical reaction was popular in Freud's day because it responded well to psychoanalysis.

Traditional psychiatry has had a spectacular lack of success with alcoholism. The premise that excessive drinking is caused by unresolved conflicts led to the hypothesis that exploring and resolving these conflicts would result in alleviation of the destructive drinking. It is possible that this hypothesis is correct, but patients keep dying of cirrhosis, pancreatitis, and ulcers before their conflicts can be resolved.

Because alcoholics did not respond well to treatment, and because alcoholics are noted for their virtuosity at frustrating and infuriating those who try to help them, psychiatry defined alcoholism out of the field of mental health by viewing alcoholics as too resistant for therapy. Until very recently alcoholism treatment was left to Alcoholics Anonymous, a self-help group which has a number of significant advantages over psychiatry in its approach to alcoholism: First, it costs nothing to the alcoholic, the state, or insurance companies. Second, the program consists of recovering alcoholics who expect in their members the kind of behavior that alienates professionals. A.A. members, because they are alcoholics themselves, can neutralize a primary device that alcoholics employ to keep themselves isolated and helpless: their negative self-judgment. Because a chronic alcoholic thinks of himself as worthless, he imagines that nonalcoholics are judgmental, moral paragons with no use for someone like him. And in fact it is usually quite easy for a professional alcoholic to train other people to meet his expectations. However, another alcoholic, who may be able to match the first in repeated acts of self-destruction, can avoid being cast in the role of judge.

The most important advantages A.A. has over the medical profession, however, are these: the members of A.A. are there to help themselves and no one else, and are, therefore, less likely to value themselves in proportion to the success they have with "patients." And most important, A.A. focuses on drinking behavior rather than its motivation. The organization encourages its members to stop drinking regardless of why they started. The members are told that they can work out troublesome aspects of their personality later—when they are sober.

Drunkenness might be defined as a state of intoxication sufficiently extreme to be immediately noticeable to nine out of ten people. Most people find such a state unpleasant; indeed, most people avoid drunkenness. It is physically unpleasant, with the possibility of headache and nausea, and it is socially, legally, and physically dangerous as well.

Yet, as we all know, people reach this state all the time. In my training workshops, the first question I ask is, "Why do people get drunk?" In light of what has already been said, this is not a fair question. It is very difficult to determine reliably why anyone does anything, and even if it were possible, the information would be of dubious value. Nevertheless, pondering this question helps workshop participants to experience the difference in usefulness between "why" questions and "what happens" questions. It also forces them to do some serious critical thinking in an area where they assume they already know the answers.

The answer that comes up most often in these workshops is, "People get drunk to escape problems or pain or bad feelings." This answer seems obvious until it is examined. The need to escape from one's problems and anxieties is universal. Escape is not only desirable, but healthy and necessary. When I ask my workshop groups why they do not use alcohol for escape, there are many different responses, but they seem to concentrate in two areas:

1. The price is too high. Whatever relief alcohol may afford is outweighed by such side effects as hangover and other physical discomfort, or by the risk of embarrassment or injury.

2. It doesn't work: Alcohol is not an effective agent of escape. It provides some distraction, but it is quite possible that a drinker might continue to brood about problems while drinking. In addition, drinking, while not contributing to the solution of problems, is quite likely to cause even more problems and bad feelings.

In the experience of most people, therefore, alcohol is not a useful tool of escape from either an economic or utilization point of view. It costs too much and it doesn't work. Related hypotheses such as analgesia or a seeking of oblivion can be dismissed with the same objections.

The other major psychodynamic hypothesis is harder to dismiss. This is the notion that people become drunk out of a need for self-punishment. Undoubtedly, such a need exists in many people. There are too many examples of behavior that can reasonably be explained by supposing that a person has sentenced himself for crimes or transgressions known or unknown.

But this leaves unanswered the question of why one would choose drunkenness as the specific agent of justice. What particular features of drunkenness attract those self-punishment enthusiasts who might otherwise be drawn to gambling, accidents, working in human services, or other self-flagellatory pastimes? Unless we can discover this, the theory is useless.

If we move outside the individual to observe drunken behavior and its impact on others, we can derive a set of hypotheses that is somewhat harder to dismiss. Some people maintain that drunkenness enables people to act without responsibility. In order to discuss this, it is important to distinguish between assigned and accepted responsibility. The sense of accepted responsibility, that is, the responsibility one accepts for one's own behavior, is often radically altered by drunkenness. Many people consistently accept drunkenness as a valid self-defense. It is also true, however, that people generally have little trouble justifying their own behavior, even without chemical assistance. Thus drunkenness hardly seems necessary to avoid responsibility.

Assigned responsibility, i.e., being held responsible by others for one's actions, is often disallowed in a subtle way by drunkenness. In both legal and interpersonal contexts, drunkenness is often accepted as a mitigating circumstance. If, after all, a drunk calls you a jerk, it is because he is drunk. If a sober person does the same, it may be because you are, in fact, a jerk. So it is easier to forgive the drunk. Often, however, one is forced to bear full responsibility for drunken behavior, generally accompanied by guilt and self-reprisal. To depend on drunkenness to protect us from the judgment of our fellows or institutions is precarious indeed.

The hypothesis with which I am most comfortable and which seems most consistent with the available data is the notion that people get drunk in order to become powerful in interpersonal contexts. It is, of course, impossible to read minds (or at least impossible to convince the scientific community that mind reading is an acceptable way to gather data). And because mind reading may be the only way to get truly dependable information about motivation, it is wise to be highly suspicious of any explanation of why any human behavior occurs. (In fact, a good case could be made that the entire concept of causality is a notion best avoided by therapists or agents of change in general.)

It is far more useful to observe what happens before and after a given behavior occurs. When discernible patterns are observed to repeat over and over again, to the point where an observer can dependably predict the rest of a sequence from seeing the early moves in a pattern, then one has information which is well organized for planning an intervention. So then, *what* happens when someone becomes drunk? Unlike the "why" question, this one can be answered, and the answer is this: that person becomes disproportionately powerful in social systems in which he or she interacts.

Powerful how? Power, as defined here, is the ability to dictate the context in which behavior occurs. The manner in which a person who is drunk can do this is a phenomenon that nearly everyone has experienced—and will almost certainly experience again. The following sequence might occur as you are waiting for a bus. Out of nowhere a person throws his arm over your shoulder and begins to comment on the headlines of a newspaper you were reading, possibly keeping his face about four inches from yours, giving you an opportunity to guess what brand of liquor he has been drinking.

As we freeze this scene, we can ask a group of observers: Who is in charge? and What are the options of the person waiting for the bus? The answers are obvious.

When I (playing the role of the person who is drunk) demonstrate this scene to workshop groups, the answer is unanimous—the drunk is in charge. I have never failed to dominate the person who volunteers for the victim's role regardless of the age, sex, size, or training of the victim. And this in spite of the fact that I clearly warn the group that I am looking for a volunteer "to be manipulated for a few seconds."

The arrogance of the above boast is calculated to challenge the audience to be extremely critical of the idea that an intoxicated person controls another person with his drunkenness. The role play graphically demonstrates how helpless people feel when presented with drunkenness. Once after the demonstration I was informed that the man I had abused held a second-degree black belt in karate. Even such a formidable armament as this fails to protect one from the power of the drunk. The only options open to the victim are: (1) Try to reason with the drunk; (2) forcefully, even physically, confront the drunk; (3) wait until the drunk goes away, like the flu.

Option one, reasoning with the drunk, is excellent if it works, but its success is so unlikely that hardly anyone tries it. Option two, forceful confrontation, is extremely risky, with a dubious payoff. People when drunk are notoriously dangerous (over two-thirds of murders involve drunkenness), especially if you consider that winning a fight with a drunk can be as dangerous as losing one. The karate expert, for instance, would be at a serious legal risk if the other person were injured. Even if we ignore the above facts, the fact that one finds oneself in such a fight is *prima facie* evidence that the intoxicated person has control of the context of interaction: no one in his right mind looks for a fight with a drunk. Option three, waiting for the drunk to go away, is the most popular tactic. The frequency of this passive response to being abused underlines who has the power in the situation.

There is a fourth option, one that affords a good chance of sending the offending person on his way in peace. This strategy will be discussed later. First, let's continue looking at the power dynamics of drunkenness.

Most people have experienced how one drunken individual can control large numbers of people at once. A person who is raving at a restaurant or party can focus all energy and attention upon himself, while simultaneously paralyzing the entire group. The age, sex, intelligence, social class, race, and so forth, of the person who is drunk or his victim are largely irrelevant. What is relevant is the fact of drunkenness. Because nearly everyone has experienced this phenomenon at one time or another and because these effects can be reproduced at any time, it is hard to dismiss the premise that drunkenness produces heightened interpersonal power. So while we may not be able to establish that people get drunk to get powerful, we can establish that people get powerful when they get drunk.

But back to the original question, "Why do people get drunk?" Traditional social science attempts to establish motivation by projective psychological testing. There is the story (perhaps apocryphal) that after World War II the army was so concerned about alcoholism that it commissioned a group of psychologists to test alcoholics to get a profile of the "alcoholic personality." Thousands of alcoholic and nonalcoholic men were put through an exhaustive battery of personality tests.

After careful analysis it was found that the alcoholic group drank significantly more than the nonalcoholic group.

While this story is a favorite among workers in alcoholism, there are studies that show significant differences between alcoholic and nonalcoholic populations. One prominent investigator, David C. McClelland, devised a test to show how concerned a subject is with power. Not surprisingly, the alcoholic population scored significantly higher in power concerns than a nonalcoholic control group. A. A. Sorenson replicated these results in a study of clergy in a paper, "Need for Power Among Alcoholic and Nonalcoholic Clergy," published in the *Journal for the Scientific Study of Religion* in 1972. The above are cited to demonstrate some mainstream scientific acceptance of the link between drunkenness and power. If, indeed, alcohol is a specific medicine for feelings of powerlessness and inadequacy, then the popularity of drunkenness becomes more understandable.

The clinical implications of this link will be explored later. First it seems important to look at how the alcoholic's power operates in a working group rather than among strangers.

Let us imagine a professional group in a large mental health agency, although the same principles would apply in any group that consistently works together. The team consists of, say, twelve therapists of varying training, experience, and tenure with the group.

The leader of this team, Dr. X, has held his position for two years. Dr. X is a private person who does not socialize with his colleagues outside the agency; nevertheless he is quite popular and is generally considered to be competent. A few of the therapists serving under him consider themselves close to him; others respect him as a professional. Dr. X has many responsibilities within the group. He does most of the clinical supervision, he assigns cases that have been through intake, he interprets policy from higher administration and brings the concerns of the group to policy level, and he has many other minor duties typical of the director of a team.

At nine o'clock every Monday morning there is a team

meeting. It is the most important meeting of the week, the time reserved for assigning of new cases, consultation on troublesome cases, updating the team on the vagaries of higher administration, problem solving on issues confronting the team, and generally starting the week with a sense of contact and control.

One Monday morning Dr. X is a few minutes late, and everyone is seated when he arrives. The few steps he takes between the door and his seat plus his manner of sitting down are sufficient data for everyone on the team to realize that he is drunk. No one at the meeting has any information about his drinking. Eyes dart around the room, and everyone hopes that someone will know what to do. "Lotta work t'do today. Who's got the first case?" Dr. X says, slurring his words.

What are the options available to the group?

When this problem is presented to workshop groups, participants are invited to brainstorm alternatives, reserving analysis until the end. The results of this brainstorming vary from group to group, but the following list includes all but the most bizarre alternatives:

1. Ignore and continue as if nothing is wrong (always mentioned first).
2. Confront (directly call attention to the problem)
   a. angrily ("What do you mean coming to work like that?")
   b. humorously ("Wow, you must be feeling no pain.")
   c. with concern ("Gosh, X, is there something bothering you?")
   d. indirectly ("Golly, Z, what's wrong with Dr. X? He looks sick.").
3. Get up and leave.
4. Join in (abandon all hope of working and socialize).
5. Cancel the meeting.
6. Get help (from X's wife or friend).
7. Concoct a ruse or subterfuge to get Dr. X to leave so the group can meet without him.

8. Report Dr. X to his superior.
9. Suggest to Dr. X that he drink a lot of coffee.
10. Exclude Dr. X from the meeting; continue without him.

When no further alternatives can be wrung from a group, I try to point out that these represent all the alternatives a group of professional communicators and problem solvers can conjure up to deal with this situation. Drunkenness affords few attractive options.

These possible responses can then be analyzed by five criteria (developed by various groups over the years). The first is: Does the work get done? It is understood that there is a great deal of short-term pressure on this hypothetical mental health team to get the job done. Clients who have had intake interviews must be assigned, troublesome cases must be discussed, administrative decisions must be explained.

The second consideration is how a chosen alternative will affect the feelings of the team members. Some of the options mentioned will be more emotionally painful to some or all of the members than other options.

The third criterion is how the future of the team as a working unit will be affected by the alternative taken. Certain moves will tend to factionalize and alienate the team; some may even threaten its existence.

Fourth we must consider how much an alternative depends on Dr. X's cooperation for its success. Obviously any alternative can be effective if Dr. X allows it to be. But we must take into account that one of the most consistent effects of drunkenness is to make the behavior of the person affected less predictable.

Finally we must consider the message, overt or covert, that Dr. X will recieve about the team's reaction to his behavior. This of course is hard to predict. It is hard enough to forecast confidently how a sober person will interpret the actions of others; predicting what a person who is drunk will deduce is next to impossible. However, there are certain reasonable predictions that can be made. For instance, if the team were to adopt option number one and pretend not to notice Dr. X's condition, it is reasonable to suppose he might infer that they failed to notice anything different and so the alcohol was not altering his functioning. Such a conclusion would make it easy for him to rationalize a repeat performance. More relevent criteria may occur to the reader, but the five we have will give us a start.

The thought of analyzing ten (actually thirteen) alternatives against five criteria seems a formidable task. Fortunately, there are some shortcuts available. One is to eliminate as unfeasible those alternatives which either involve or might lead to some form of confrontation.

At first this suggestion may seem a bit high-handed and precipitous. Many workshop participants strenuously object, especially those who have been trained in confrontational therapy styles or those who come from alcoholic families and are infuriated by drunken behavior. Even the most vociferous and indignant objectors, however, are calmed by two simple questions. The first is, "Has anyone here ever attempted to communicate in a meaningful way with a person who is drunk?" The second is, "How did it go?"

These questions serve to remind the group that people who are drunk do not abide by the standard rules of communication. The probable outcomes of directly calling attention to Dr. X's condition are: an argument between Dr. X and various members of the team; or a therapy session conducted by members of the team upon Dr. X. It is hard to see either as a productive use of time and emotional energy. Or, by our aforementioned criteria: (1) the work won't get done; (2) everyone will feel frustrated and exploited; (3) the team will fracture into at least two and possibly three groups—namely, those who are angrily (or concernedly) confronting Dr. X, those who think the confronters are too insensitve (or too sympathetic) to Dr. X's situation, and finally those who resent both of the other groups for wasting everyone's time talking to Dr. X at all. (I would find myself firmly committed to the last group.) (4) Clearly the success of this option depends on Dr.

X's cooperation, which is at best unreliable. (5) One could bet that the message Dr. X is likely to get from being argued with or therapized by his staff will not be particularly beneficial.

Apart from the foregoing, calling attention openly to Dr. X's condition violates two rules I've developed for comfortable and effective communication, to wit: Never fight a drunk and Never shrink a drunk. I rest my case. These rules apply not only to alternative number two (a, b, c, d) but to number three, number five, and number ten as well. How, we will discuss.

Let us consider the option of joining in—i.e., realizing that no work is going to get done and turning the meeting into a social occasion. Whereas this may assuage the feelings of some of the members, it will certainly irritate others (possibly including Dr. X) to an impressive degree. The work certainly will not get done, and Dr. X may feel that the team welcomes his ebullient new self (if, of course, he goes along. If he doesn't, then the team runs the risk of a confrontation).

The idea of getting outside help is attractive until one realizes that this merely adds new members to the team. There is absolutely no guarantee that a wife or friend will be more effective than anyone else. It is additionally possible that Dr. X may be infuriated by the effrontery of calling people from his personal life into his work space—especially if he denies being drunk.

A ruse or subterfuge to lure Dr. X out of the room also has a shiny initial attraction until one starts to ask logistical questions like "How?" Or just as important, "Where?" "By whom?" "What then?"

Any ruse suffers from the possibility of what might happen when Dr. X discovers that he has been deceived. A calm and sober person might be expected to become furious under the circumstances; what of a person who is drunk?

Where do you take him? If another member of the clinic staff sees him, stories may begin which endanger the existence of the team. Who is going to accept the martyr's role of being seen with Dr. X—or of deceiving him? How do you keep him out of the meeting? This one is much trickier than it at first appears. The team would be ill advised to pin its hopes on this style of deceit.

Which brings us to the alternative of reporting Dr. X to his superior. Many workshop groups do not even list this among the alternatives. I usually add it to the list, joking that the group must be too kind to have thought of it. Actually, I suspect the absence of this option is due more to wisdom than kindness.

Reporting Dr. X to his superior does not solve the immediate problem of what to do at the meeting. But even beyond this, the person who reports Dr. X is doing Dr. X's supervisor the favor of presenting him or her with much the same attractive options available to the team. It is unlikely that the supervisor will be grateful.

It is reasonable to assume that, because Dr. X is considered popular and competent, and because this is the first instance of such behavior, the decision to turn Dr. X in will be far from unanimous. Some people may feel that such an action is extreme and disloyal, perhaps even spiteful. It would not be surprising if some team members ascribed ignoble motives to the reporter, especially if that person could be considered a rival of Dr. X.

But the person reporting Dr. X will probably have supporters as well, and these supporters might also have strong feelings. People who have previous experience with alcoholism in someone close might react with intense anger toward the drunkenness. In any case, it is not overly pessimistic to suppose that the team might divide into at least two factions exchanging ideas in an atmosphere of limited mutual respect.

Attention must also be paid to the fate of the person who reports Dr. X. As previously mentioned, there are many possible interpretations of the motivation for such an act. Even if there is general consensus that the reporter was motivated by a sincere desire to save the team, that person's survival as a team member would seem much shakier than that of Dr. X himself. In fact, regardless of the fate of Dr. X, it is hard to imagine circumstances under which the reporter could comfortably continue as a team member.

Experience with analogous situations would indicate that Dr. X might well continue as team leader. It has already been hinted that Dr. X's supervisor has options scarcely more attractive than those confronting the team. The supervisor can fire Dr. X summarily. This may be the best option in the long run, but it has serious long- and short-term liabilities. Along with making the statement that Dr. X's behavior is intolerable, the supervisor is also metacommunicating that one serious mistake is fatal in the agency and that the agency, which is in the business of helping sick people, treats illness among its staff as a crime. It would not be surprising if there were strong feelings both for and against this action in the agency as a whole—not just in Dr. X's team.

The supervisor can warn Dr. X that a repeat of his behavior will mean dismissal, perhaps also demanding that Dr. X seek treatment. This option has some actual long-term promise. It is certainly recommended by many experts as *the* method of dealing with drunkenness on the job. However, in this context, as in any other, there are serious liabilities.

The first one that may occur to Dr. X's supervisor is that what may have been a warm, collegial relationship will be changed into a parole officer–parolee dynamic. But even if the supervisor, Dr. S, is willing to accept this responsibility, it is not at all certain that S. can enforce the threat. The problems of the option of firing Dr. X are not canceled by a warning or ultimatum.

Even more important is consideration of the functioning of Dr. X's team. He is in a position where his judgment and his team's faith in it are key factors in his functioning. The problem of how, or even if, Dr. X's subordinates should share the way in which the situation is being handled would take some thought. Both keeping the information secret or telling all would, in different ways, damage Dr. X and the team's working relationship.

If the supervisor decides not to inform the team of the status of their leader, it will appear to the team members that the incident is being ignored and staff morale suffers. The reporter took a major risk in informing those in authority—and nothing happened. If, however, the team is informed of the warning to Dr. X, they become allied with their boss's supervisor in the task of enforcing the ultimatum. Dr. X becomes a boss, a supervisor, a charge, and a patient to this staff. It is hard to see how the team can operate adequately under the burden of this cross-hierarchial alliance.

The team will also have to contend with the very human problem of knowing that Dr. X's job, perhaps even his career, is on the line. If Dr. X transgresses, to report him would mean his certain ruin. The pressure to become a rescuing conspiracy will be considerable. If such a conspiracy forms, then to inform Dr. X later would be to inform on the unprofessional silence of the rest of the team as well.

It is easy to imagine the supervisor with this maze of options, possibilities, and political ramifications beginning to find option number three attractive: to waffle. This would not necessarily mean ignoring or denying the incident, and it might mean failure to react clearly and decisively, leaving Dr. X and his staff with little idea of the official position regarding the incident. Such a state of affairs typically produces a state of paralysis, frustration, and eventually cynicism in everyone.

So our afflicted team, inviting the above, still ponders an appropriate response to the behavior of their erstwhile trusted leader. They will find their remaining options no more alluring than those already examined. Any attempt to postpone or cancel the meeting or to exclude Dr. X can be interpreted by Dr. X as a challenge to his authority that might precipitate a confrontation.

Any member attempting to leave the meeting could be challenged by Dr. X. Even if some members escape without incident, the remaining members are likely to resent being left with a difficult situation. Those who leave could virtuously point out that those who remain are condoning Dr. X's behavior. The resulting exchange of ideas might lead to enhanced understanding and communication among the members of the team. It might not. In any case, it would not bring the team any closer to a solution. In fact, without cooperative and rational behavior on the part of Dr. X (a sanguine assumption, at best) none of the options hold much promise. Which brings us back to option number one, ignoring Dr. X's behavior.

Denial has long suffered from a bad press in the field of mental health. Freud labeled it the most primitive of defense mechanisms, and alcoholism workers justly consider it their most potent enemy. In such an atmosphere it is sometimes difficult to understand its attraction. If, however, we take the time to analyze our alternatives, denial's popularity becomes less mysterious.

If the team decides not to refer directly to Dr. X's condition and carry on with the meeting as best it can, the work may get done after a fashion. The feelings of the team members will be tried, but if there are no dramatic flare-ups and teamwork is close, they might have a feeling of accomplishment under duress (as well as release from the concern that would exist with other options). The team would avoid a crisis that might endanger its survival. And, while it is true that this option would also require the cooperation of Dr. X, it does not demand that Dr. X admit that something is wrong, which makes his cooperation easier to count on.

A serious drawback to option number one is the fact that it tacitly approves of Dr. X's behavior and makes it more likely to recur. The team can easily rationalize that their sanction has no impact on Dr. X's behavior. Also, given Dr. X's obvious lack of consideration for their feelings, the team may not be able to consider the full effect their action will have on Dr. X's continued sobriety. If in fact the team chooses option number one, it is possible that everything will come out all right, as will be discussed later. In any case, option number one, even if not a clear favorite, is hard to dismiss, given the alternatives.

When the team chooses option number one, as most teams

in this circumstance will, it will have to make some necessary structural changes in order to carry on the meeting and protect its interests: In short, the team will have to covertly redistribute Dr. X's functions among the other members. Imagine, for instance, that one of the members presents an intake. Dr. X after a conspicuous pause sways and says: "It is dangerous to continue seeing the adolescent without bringing in the family."

Now this may be good advice, but what is most important to remember about Dr. X's functioning is that there is no way of evaluating his communications. So whereas Dr. X's advice might be sound, there is no way the presenter can assume it is sound or even that Dr. X can be held responsible for it. No one, in addition, wants to be held responsible for acting on the advice of a person who is drunk, so the presenter of the case has a problem, as would anyone else who presents.

Another team member could alter the situation by saying something like "Yes, and I think it's very important how we present the idea of family therapy to the youngster." Most clinical teams have an unofficial hierarchy of experience and competence in different areas. If the top person in the hierarchy is not available, the team will look to the next one down. When Dr. X's advice is either supported or subtly amended by a respected member of the team, the presenter has a basis on which to act.

Later in the meeting when some information has to be delivered to the administration, Dr. X, who usually does this, says he will deliver it. However, the team cannot depend on Dr. X. He *may* deliver the information, but it would be incorrect to assume he will, so another team member might casually say, "Oh, I'm going up there right after the meeting; I'll take it up, and while I'm there I might as well ask them about those other matters we had questions about." And so on.

This could be a smooth process if Dr. X had an assistant, or if he had had an extended previous absence which forced the team to redelegate his functions. Neither is the case here, and the team faces a difficult, halting, uncomfortable process. If they pull it off, they can be justifiably proud. But it must be said that however difficult, this restructuring is absolutely necessary to the functioning of the team and however painful, is significantly less painful than any other available alternative.

As the team files out of the conference room filled with conflicting emotions, it should be noted that the fate of the group has yet to be determined. Only when Dr. X gets a chance to explain his actions can we determine what happens to this team. Actually there are only two possibilities. The first—certainly the most desirable—is that when Dr. X is sober—perhaps the next day—a team member who has private access to Dr. X will say something like, "Hey, what was wrong with you yesterday? You sure seemed off your game."

To which Dr. X might reply, "God, I'm so embarrassed. I met an old army buddy last night and we went out drinking. At five o'clock in the morning I woke up in his house with a hangover. I had a lot to do at the meeting, and I was so messed up that I thought I should just have a hair of the dog and come in rather than call in sick. I must have been crazy. Did everyone know?"

At this point everyone on the team has permission to deal directly with the incident. Dr. X will almost certainly be the recipient of some anger and punishment. The team may be suspicious for a while, but if the incident is not repeated, the team will probably regain its former level of functioning and the incident will become an amusing part of the team's common lore.

However, Dr. X could reply to the question, "Oh, I was just a little tired," and then actively resist further probing, thus placing the questioner in the position of backing down or calling him a liar. At that moment an alcoholic system is born.

Now there are other available scenarios. Dr. X could reply as in the first example but later repeat the incident. Or he might offer a lame excuse that denies responsibility for his behavior. Or he might deny that he was functioning at less-than-peak efficiency. The result will be the same—an alcoholic system in which the team knows that they can no longer trust Dr. X's communications and, even if he never comes in drunk again, the dynamic and structure of the team is irredeemably altered.

When, through one of the processes described above, the team realizes that Dr. X's role has permanently changed, certain structural changes become inevitable. The most obvious of these is isolation; the team recognizes that many of their processes cannot be safely shared with the outside world. If, indeed, they decide not to report Dr. X or make information about his behavior available to nonteam members, they become accessories to his behavior, and each member receives an invisible membership card in a conspiracy of silence. It must become more and more obvious to team members that anyone outside the team who learns the secret has the power to radically alter the team's functioning, if not to destroy it.

Even within the team, communication becomes constrained. The unpredictability of Dr. X plus the danger of communicating clearly in his presence make boundaries unclear. No one can be sure what it is now safe to say. The power structure of the team has become so covert and unclear that a comment about Dr. X or even about how someone else is responding to Dr. X, might be interpreted as a power play. If one can no longer criticize Dr. X, how can one accept criticism or even feedback from colleagues? No one has the clear right to set limits, define boundaries, or enforce standards. Everyone on the team, by reason of his or her silence and inaction, now shares Dr. X's guilt, and the guilty are unlikely to invite a judge.

In a system with no clear boundaries, closeness is impossible. To take a clear and public position makes one vulnerable and threatening to the rest of the group, without providing the usual payoff of power and clarity. Therefore communication must go underground. The explicit becomes tacit. It is predictable that the energy level in such a system will drop, as will the self-esteem of its membership.

As the team members become increasingly isolated from each other, and as the team's internal communication becomes more tense and circuitous, with a concomitant drop in energy and self-esteem, each member faces three alternatives: to precipitate crisis and a resulting change, to leave the team, or to stay and try to make things as tolerable as possible.

The option of precipitating change has already been analyzed in part as we examined the options available to the team. As unattractive as moves which might precipitate crisis seem at first, they lose even more appeal as time goes on, and each member of the team has already tacitly put himself or herself on record as having accepted the situation. Moreover, as a person's energy level and self-esteem erode, that person is less likely to have the resources to make dramatic moves.

This also applies to the option of leaving the team. There may well be a deluge of résumés from the team offices as matters begin to deteriorate, but eroded confidence and self-esteem make it difficult to seek or find new employment. Some team members will leave, but this fact could further undermine the energy and self-esteem of those who remain. Those who stay must confront the problem of making the best of a tense and unsatisfying situation. All therapists, whether they work in a physical or emotional context, are familiar with the phenomenon of the secondary gain.

Everything cuts both ways. No event is so positive that it is without significant negative aspects and no affliction is without its compensation. For example, the person struck with cancer finds that people are more considerate and supportive—less demanding and judgmental. It becomes much easier to set priorities and focus effort. Whereas cancer is an extremely high price to pay for these benefits, the cancer patient is ill advised to ignore them. There are enough negative aspects to the condition that maximizing the secondary gains seems like a natural way to counteract despair. So it is with people living in a pathological system. The secondary gains are all there are, so one is forced to develop a taste for them. (This is not to say that the taste may not already be developed, and that some may actively, if unconsciously, seek situations where they are likely to be on the menu. More on this later.)

Therefore, membership in Dr. X's team is not without its

compensations, and it might be useful to examine some of these. In the late Middle Ages, the Church found the practice of selling indulgences profitable. Buying an indulgence meant purchasing forgiveness for all earthly sins, and although the price was steep—all of the customer's wordly possessions—it was worth it for many people. Although the Church no longer handles this particular product, the market still exists. Many of us are unsure enough of our virtue that some incontestable evidence of our blamelessness would be welcome.

On Dr. X's team everyone has an indulgence. If anything goes wrong, and it is safe to say that plenty will, everyone on the team knows where the blame can be placed. This is well understood within the team, but outsiders are not aware of the existence of a general indulgence. Team members may experience the additional virtue of being martyred for the transgressions of another, nobly forbearing to speak while unjust punishment is meted out.

Related to this is the fact that the team must redistribute Dr. X's duties in order to function even at a minimal level. This, of course, means that some members have, in addition to their own full-time responsibilities, significant unofficial and uncompensated tasks. These extra duties are more difficult to discharge than they would be if officially assigned because they include the additional burden of deception.

While there is a certain thanklessness about these tasks, there is some balance. Let us imagine that Ms. Y covertly replaces Dr. X's function as clinical supervisor. The team has learned to look to her for experienced advice on difficult cases. If Mr. Z is having a problem with a case and presents it at a meeting, everyone will wait patiently while Dr. X raves on. If he chooses to speak, then Ms. Y will give her views. These will effectively replace Dr. X's views in the old structure; they will be taken as the authoritative word.

If Ms. Y's advice works out well, she gets the satisfaction of doing work on a much higher level than is officially recognized. She has a chance to try out and polish supervisory skills in a familiar, low-risk context. The satisfaction of success (other than material) is perhaps even higher than if it were really her job to supervise: After all, the team listens to her, not because of her job title, but because she has been covertly elected first among peers.

The risks are low indeed. If her advice doesn't work out, her self-esteem (consciously at least) is defended on three levels. It is not her job to supervise in the first place. Dr. X's behavior has made everything impossible anyway, and the best of advice can be mangled in its execution, especially when one does not have administrative power to enforce one's judgment. The result of this dynamic is that Ms. Y finds herself enjoying a great deal of power and influence for which she is not readily accountable in the system. Anything that goes wrong is still Dr. X's fault. In some ways you might say that Ms. Y gets power without responsibility, as does a person who is drunk (without the risk to her liver or her reputation).

Ms. Y, of course, is not the only person for whom the foregoing process occurs. It happens in a different way for each member of the team. Dr. X's behavior removes the risk of failure and defeat for all team members. In the words of the gambler in the film *The Hustler,* he gives them an excuse to lose.

In a system where the usual ways of meeting needs are unavailable, secondary gains become the coin of the realm. In *Getting Well Again,* Carl and Stephanie Simonton consider secondary gains of cancer patients simply as new means of meeting real needs. They consider it vital for the patients to find strategies that don't require illness for meeting these needs. There is nothing wrong with the needs, but only with the expense of getting them met through cancer. To move back to our example, Ms. Y has a legitimate need for a safe place to try out new skills and permission not to blame herself if things go wrong, but she is paying an exorbitant price to meet these needs as a member of Dr. X's team. When people must sacrifice their self-esteem in order to meet legitimate human needs, they are members of a pathological system.

2

The Bottle
as Trainer:
The Development
of an Alcoholic Family

In the previous chapter an analogy between a mental health team and a family was drawn, but in important ways these are not completely analogous situations. One obvious difference is the degree and quality of commitment and membership. When things go badly in a family, members do not flood the mails with résumés looking for new families. An organization can change its membership to meet changing needs or situations. A family's membership is permanent, and the depth of emotional commitment is clearly different.

Another important difference is that the rules, structure, roles, and expectations of an agency or business tend to be much more conscious and defined than in a family system. This is so because the goals of organizations are usually more clearly and easily defined by a consensus. If, for example, one were to ask a family "What is your goal?" it is likely that one would get myriad diverse answers, probably followed by an argument. In an agency or business, the system's organizational goals are usually neatly printed in the annual report.

This is not to say that all of the goals, roles, or processes of an agency or business are defined or conscious, but at least the membership can be held accountable to those that are.

A third and very important difference has to do with the

context of drunkenness. As most alcoholism literature makes clear, problematic use of alcohol is not defined by frequency or amount of use but by the *context* of use. If, for example, a surgeon performs a difficult operation and has three drinks afterward, that surgeon may simply be unwinding. If the surgeon has three drinks and then performs a difficult operation, the surgeon is an alcoholic. People who cannot limit their use of alcohol to contexts in which it is safe and appropriate are clearly problem drinkers. In a work context, where the use of alcohol is rarely appropriate, it is far easier to define drinking as problematic. In the home there are more contexts in which the use of alcohol is accepted. This makes it much harder to define a drinking behavior as problematic. It is also true, however, that recognition of a family member's drinking as problematic leaves a family with the same alternatives which presented themselves to Dr. X's team. And this is not a particularly attractive conclusion to reach.

In any case it can be safely stated that as difficult as it is for a working team to cope successfully with drunkenness in a key member, it is even more difficult for a family. A family has more emotional involvement and fewer options. Before we look at what happens in an alcoholic family, it is necessary to understand something of the nature of alcoholism.

The most important characteristic of alcoholism is that it is extremely difficult to define or diagnose in its early, or even middle, stages. For this reason one so often hears terms like "heavy drinker," "alcohol abuser," or "problem drinker." There is a clear white area of the occasional social drinker and a clear black area of the chronic detoxification patient, but the gray area in between has no clear lines of demarcation. E. M. Jellinek attempted to draw some by devising a scale that charts the stages of alcoholism. While his work is useful, many people progress some distance down the curve and then slide no farther, while others actually improve while continuing to drink. Still others suffer significant alcohol-related disabilities while hardly touching the curve at all (see Fig. 1, adapted from Jellinek Chart). Part of this ambiguity is due to the nature of the

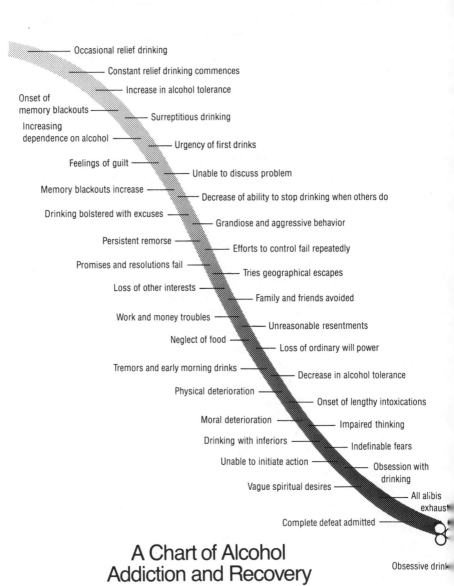

Occasional relief drinking

Constant relief drinking commences

Increase in alcohol tolerance

Onset of
memory blackouts

Surreptitious drinking

Increasing
dependence on alcohol

Urgency of first drinks

Feelings of guilt

Unable to discuss problem

Memory blackouts increase

Decrease of ability to stop drinking when others do

Drinking bolstered with excuses

Grandiose and aggressive behavior

Persistent remorse

Efforts to control fail repeatedly

Promises and resolutions fail

Tries geographical escapes

Loss of other interests

Family and friends avoided

Work and money troubles

Unreasonable resentments

Neglect of food

Loss of ordinary will power

Tremors and early morning drinks

Decrease in alcohol tolerance

Physical deterioration

Onset of lengthy intoxications

Moral deterioration

Impaired thinking

Drinking with inferiors

Indefinable fears

Unable to initiate action

Obsession with
drinking

Vague spiritual desires

All alibis
exhaus

Complete defeat admitted

Obsessive drink

A Chart of Alcohol
Addiction and Recovery

Adapted from E. M. Jellinek

Enlightened and interesting way of life opens up with road ahead to higher levels than ever before.

Group therapy and mutual help continue ——

—— Increasing tolerance

Rationalizations recognized ——

—— Contentment in sobriety

Care of personal appearance ——

—— Confidence of employers

First steps toward economic stability ——

—— Increase of emotional control

Appreciation of real values ——

—— Facts faced with courage

Rebirth of ideals ——

—— New circle of stable friends

New interests develop ——

—— Family and friends appreciate efforts

Adjustment to family needs ——

—— Natural rest and sleep

Desire to escape goes ——

—— Realistic thinking

Return of self-esteem ——

—— Regular nourishment taken

Diminishing fears of the unknown future ——

—— Appreciation of possibilities of new way of life

Start of group therapy ——

—— Onset of new hope

Physical overhaul by doctor ——

—— Spiritual needs examined

Right thinking begins ——

—— Assisted in personal stocktaking

Meets former addicts normal and happy ——

—— Stops taking alcohol

Told addiction can be arrested ——

—— Learns alcoholism is an illness

—— Honest desire for help

ontinues in vicious circles

drug itself as well as to the extremely contradictory role it occupies in our culture.

Alcohol is a central nervous system depressant, which means that it reduces the efficiency with which the nervous system can transmit signals throughout the body. All other CNS depressants are heavily controlled because they impair functioning and because they are addictive, but alcohol, because of its long history as a recreational and ceremonial drug, has a radically different image from its cousins the barbiturates, or its more efficient relatives the opiates. The fact is that any alcohol impairs neurological functioning, so the degree to which one allows oneself to be impaired depends on a subjective judgment of what is pleasurable and what is right. While we can obtain sophisticated information about the physiological and even the psychological effects of alcohol upon the individual, I am more concerned with its effects on the interactional space between individuals and the systems they form.

In order to discuss these interactions, it is necessary to digress briefly to examine the notion of the boundary, one of the key concepts in systems thinking. Simply stated, the boundary is the outline which delineates a system from its surroundings. This outline may be quite clear and distinct, like the border of a country, or it can be vague or covert, like the boundary around the system of *baseball fans*. Is a baseball fan someone who has a season ticket, or someone who occasionally takes in a ball game? This could be endlessly debated, whereas it is easier to define what we mean by *Canadian*.

The nature of the outline itself varies widely from system to system. Some boundaries require elaborate ritualized examinations of anyone passing through, like the border of a military police state, while others are relatively open and casual, like the U.S.–Canadian border. Some boundaries appear fluid and permeable, but turn out to be somewhat rigid when there is an attempt at transit.

We all find ourselves within the boundaries of many systems. Families, cliques, classes, interest groups, teams, companies, inhabitants of an office, sharers of a lunch shift—all are systems with boundaries.

A baseball team, for example, has a boundary that encloses the whole team: administrators, typists, coaches, trainers, players, and so forth. Within this group there are subsystems: front office people, players, managers, and coaches, support people—as well as less obvious subsystems, such as bull pen crew, Latin American players, bridge players, those who frequent Charlie's Bar, swinging singles, and so on.

Any person on the team may be a member of several of these subsystems, each of them having different boundaries and different rules of behavior. A Latin American player who is also a bull pen pitcher and also a bridge player would behave differently depending on which subsystem he felt part of at a particular moment. If, for example, he were socializing with other Latin American players, he might give excluding signals to other bull pen crew or bridge players with whom he feels close in other contexts. He might also enforce the boundary of the Latin American players' subsystem by continuing to speak Spanish when the friend from the bull pen arrived. The same player might exclude a Latin American player from a conversation among bull pen mates—perhaps by continuing to discuss opposing batters.

Each member of the team, then, is a member of several subsystems within the team as well as other systems that may or may not interface with the team: family, religious groups, political organizations, and ethnic groups are just a few examples. Whatever membership a team member may have in other systems, the most important boundary for each is the individual personal boundary. Each person in the world has a space which that person clarifies as personal space. Like any other boundary, that personal space has an outline which is unique in shape and character and which is communicated and enforced in widely varied ways. It is crucial to note that control of one's own personal space is a basic human need which will be met somehow, whether directly or indirectly. When, for whatever reason, this space cannot be controlled, as in a concentration camp, highly pathological systems result.

It would appear that a major function of alcohol is to alter boundaries. This statement applies not only to abuse and drunkenness, but to social use as well. Many people have boundaries too inflexible for social situations. They find it difficult to let others get close enough for informal contact or to let themselves be seen acting in a frivolous manner. They are shy and uptight. Happily for them, a boundary solvent is usually made available at most social gatherings in this country. Observing a party at which alcohol is served, one will note that early on there will be small clusters of people who know each other, but as the blood alcohol levels of the guests increase, intercourse becomes more fluid, talk louder and less controlled, and movement more dramatic; strangers exchange intimacies—the party becomes a success. If alcohol could not dissolve boundaries, a lot less of it would be sold.

It is important to understand that a successful boundary transaction is at least a bilateral operation—both parties communicate their boundaries and both recognize and observe the other's. Alcohol works on both ends. One is less likely to communicate one's boundary when drinking. Most boundary signals are quite subtle—small movements of the eyes, an almost imperceptible step back, a tightening of the mouth. We usually respond to them on a barely conscious level, sensing the discomfort of invasion and retreating until the subtle signs of comfort are flashed. Alcohol screens us from our own discomfort—its action tends to affect the highest and most delicate of our neurological functions first and then work its way down, and boundary behavior is one of the most refined of social actions. Alcohol therefore blurs our need to keep others at a distance or to respect rules that we usually enforce. This applies to group as well as individual boundaries. Weddings, for example, are functions where two families are in the process of blurring their boundaries. For the first time people may be meeting individuals and groups who will instantly become relatives. It is no wonder that ample intake of alcohol is not only tolerated but mandated at many such gatherings. Each family welcomes some chemical help to elasticize its boundary sufficiently to include the others.

Drunkenness—in addition to relaxing boundaries—also allows

people to enforce their boundaries and keep unwanted people out. This is what we saw in our previous example of the drunk at the bus stop: Extreme drunkenness is impervious to outside reason or influence, as anyone who has tried to communicate with a drunk will readily agree.

Although alcohol consumption may lead to some embarrassment, the fact that it relaxes the personal boundaries of the consumer does not cause nearly as much trouble as its effect on the ability to perceive the boundary signals of others. The intoxicated person in the first chapter is obnoxious because he cannot—or will not—perceive the signals indicating that his attentions are unwelcome. This makes alcohol a short-term cure for rejection and loneliness. This, combined with its ability to cure powerless feelings, certainly makes it seem a boon to an alienated and insecure society.

Unfortunately, these marvelous services come at a price. At first the cost is so insignificant that it seems nonexistent—a drink or two at a party or social gathering relaxes boundaries, decreases feelings of powerlessness and "gladdens the heart," and then wears off, leaving perhaps a faint fatigue or a mild headache. For many people this is as far as it goes. Some people, however, find the feelings that alcohol gives them very attractive. They might be people whose education never included skills of social intercourse or who have few other ways of feeling powerful or of enforcing their personal boundaries. They may, as some research indicates, have a genetic predilection for the drug. In any case, the fact that alcohol is a central nervous system depressant makes it a potentially dangerous substitute for social skills. This is partially because all central nervous system depressants share the property of fostering a physiological tolerance in users, so that it takes increasing amounts of the drug to produce a given effect. Therefore a person using alcohol regularly will tend to increase dosage over time. This increased dosage, although it will produce psychological effects similar to the smaller doses used earlier, generates more pronounced physiological effects, many of which are unpleasant.

An increased tolerance with the concomitant increase in dosage makes it harder to regulate the dosage to achieve particular psychological effects. For example, if a person has one drink at a social occasion, an increase to two drinks is noticeable—it increases the amount of alcohol ingested by 100 percent. If, on the other hand, a person increases intake from ten to thirteen drinks, the difference is only 33 percent, and the change is much less noticeable. A one-drink increase in the customary dose becomes almost imperceptible, and as the blood alcohol percentage rises, both self-perception and judgment become impaired, greatly increasing the chance of overdose. Alcohol overdoses tend to be extremely unpleasant physically, but in many cases the damage to self-esteem resulting from drug-affected behavior is even more damaging.

If a person uses alcohol to feel more confident, more powerful, more able to enforce boundaries, more able to make social contact, he may naturally come to rely on this chemical support to help him get along in the world. A habit of using alcohol to cope with certain situations lowers the motivation to learn alternate ways of handling those situations. If we depend on a car to get to work, we are unlikely to use more energy finding other ways to get there, unless the car stops functioning. If a person depends on alcohol to ease discomfort in certain interpersonal situations, an overdose—which might include embarrassing behavior—leads to a greater need to shore up self-esteem, confidence, and boundaries. Even though the person might recognize that his drinking is causing him harm, he knows no other way of feeling powerful, and he has a great need to feel powerful because of the blows to his self-esteem that have resulted from his drinking behavior.

The Makeup of the Alcoholic Family

While alcoholism is by no means confined to men, my experience in treating families with alcoholic mothers is limited. Most of the female alcoholics I have had an opportunity to treat were no longer living in the context of a family. There is a clear need for an examination of the family of the female alcoholic—a need which this work does not pretend to fill. In the families we will examine here, the father is the alcoholic.

Let's meet a typical alcoholic family, consisting of a father, a mother, and four children: a son sixteen, a daughter fourteen, another boy who is twelve, and a girl of ten.

A family of course is a working unit whose major task is to provide life support and socialization for its members. Different families divide the many tasks involved in various ways. Here they will be distributed according to orthodox sex-role stereotyping, simply because the vast majority of alcoholic families divide them in this way.

In this family the father has the job of bringing in the money. Like many other fathers, he also carries the primary responsibility for disciplining the children. This is not because men are better at discipline, but because the father is usually the more distant parent, and the more distant authority is usually the more effective disciplinarian. A strong teacher, for example, may send an unruly student to a weak principal. The student has had a long period of close contact with the teacher in which to observe and calibrate the teacher's moves and reactions, whereas the principal is an unknown entity, and it may be some time before the student is aware of the principal's weakness.

In addition, the father has responsibility for decision making. The extent of this, of course, varies from family to family. The father may make 95 percent of the decisions or 5 percent. He may think he is making 95 percent, while actually only making 5 percent, but decision making, or at least participating in a process through which decisions are made, is a responsibility most fathers hold in their families.

Very often the father has responsibility for maintenance. Men are expected to be mechanically competent, and consequently they often take responsibility for such tasks as changing sink washers or light switches, putting up shelves, getting the car serviced, mowing the lawn, clearing the yard, and shoveling the snow.

The father of the family usually has the job of handling interactions with important systems outside the family, particularly when conflict is likely to be part of the process. Talent being somewhat near equal, men are more effective at this than women. The reason for this, of course, lies in a society that remains sexist. A man complaining about a bill is likely to be taken more seriously when he complains than will his wife. It is wise to deplore such sexism—it is also foolish to act as though it does not exist. Most families don't.

The most important job that a father has in a family, however, is his affective role: being a loving and supportive husband and a gentle, firm, and available father. This includes indirectly teaching his children, through example, the art of being a man in a marriage, a father in a family, and a man in the world. This job is the most difficult and subtle of all. Difficult not only because the tasks involved are difficult to understand and performance of them hard to evaluate, but because the messages that American men receive about what society expects of them in this area are so conflicted.

Men are told, characteristically, that their function with their children is extremely important, yet society as a whole does not value men for this function. A man's place in the social order is determined by how successful he is in his career. Moreover, high-status careers almost invariably are ones which require almost fanatical dedication. The high-powered corporation executive, the successful doctor, the high-level lawyer and politician would almost of necessity view his home and family as a place to rest and recuperate from the outside world—not as a place in which to invest major energies. The father may have other duties and functions in a family, but these are the major components of the stereotypical male role.

The mother, characteristically, is responsible for children, housekeeping, quartermastering, the budget, administration, transport, purchasing, and coordinating social events. She has, of course, decision-making responsibilities and major disciplinary duties under the "children" heading. (Father was listed as having primary responsibility for discipline because he usually acts as the "heavy" for the mother, who typically handles the bulk of everyday "corrections." It is difficult to combine the nurturing and disciplining roles easily, as any single parent could testify.)

Needless to say, the mother's most important job is also affective. She must be a loving and supportive wife and a loving, stable, and nurturing mother. The importance of the nurturing role is often minimized, because this is the function most often sacrificed when the system is under pressure and resources are stretched. As we shall see, this tendency to overlook emotional considerations during an emergency or crisis often undermines seemingly well-functioning families. The body must be preserved to make the emotions relevant, but in the long run the price of ignoring emotional needs can be very high.

We have then an oversimplified description of the basic parental functions in an American family of broadly middle-class values. While it is true that in many families children consistently perform vital functions, this is not typical. Some families, particularly those of black, Latin, Chinese, and other minority cultures, still maintain an extended family structure with more than two generations living together. This allows parental functions to be distributed more flexibly and gives the family more options in an emergency. This model, though more efficient, has largely given way in this country to the nuclear family structure and will not be analyzed in this work.

These parental roles have been delineated in order to show what happens in a family when the father becomes alcoholic— that is, begins to drink in a way that consistently impairs his functioning in the family.

The Pragmatics of Drunkenness

Let us imagine that the father begins to evidence drunkenness at home with some consistency. The degree of consistency need only be such that other members of the family can no longer reasonably have confidence in his being able to act functionally at any given time. It is not that he must be drunk and dysfunctional often, only that the boundaries and rules governing drunkenness become unclear. Once the family can no longer *assume* that the father is competent and responsible, certain hard choices become necessary. To make this more clear, we can speculate on alcoholism's possible effects on the father's delineated duties.

Dad's most conspicuous task—that of procuring money for the family—is likely to be the least affected in the early stages of alcoholism. It is a rare alcoholism counselor who gets through a day without hearing the statement "I can't be an alcoholic, I've been at work every morning for the past X years."

In this culture a man's right to be a respected member of the community is largely determined by his ability to work and produce money. When a man does not do this, he slips below the minimum standard and becomes widely acknowledged as marginal. So pervasive is this value that most jobless men join society in its low opinion of them. Just as a minimum requirement of women in this culture is their ability to care for their children, the man's is to hold a job. When drinking threatens these abilities, an alcoholic reaches a choice point: to change or become a marginal member of society—a full-time professional drunk. Few alcoholics, when faced with this choice, opt for professional status.

Also, a man often has a better chance of feeling powerful and competent in his work space than at home. Roles and requirements tend to be clearer, and time structure is provided. Men in general get better training at being competent in jobs than in intimate relationships, and many men who are drinking dysfunctionally at home are simultaneously performing well at work, because they feel no need for remedial medication in the work environment.

It is generally accepted that the workplace is one of the last places to be invaded by drunkenness. Even when this happens, and statistics on industrial losses due to drunkenness attest that it does happen with disastrous frequency, the man is unlikely to be confronted or disciplined, for reasons which have already been outlined.

It is also true, however, that an alcoholic's economic functioning is unlikely to improve. Promotions will come more slowly, if at all. Layoff will be more frequent, if union rules make that possible. If a job is left, it is less likely to be replaced by a better one. In spite of the fact that the economic area is one of the last areas to decay in many cases of alcoholism, the illness is likely to put economic pressure on the family, and the pressure is likely to increase with time.

The job of disciplining the children, on the other hand, usually shows the damage promptly. There are innumerable theories of child discipline, but if there is any premise that unites almost all the theoreticians, it is the value of consistency. No matter how bizarre the content of a structure of discipline, it will tend to regulate behavior effectively if consistently enforced. Given the fact that the most consistent factor in drunken behavior is its unpredictability, it is safe to assume that drunkenness will be very disabling to a parent trying to enforce discipline.

If, for example, a teenage boy comes in after curfew several nights running, his father may:

While sober, call attention to the behavior, impose appropriate and related sanctions, and clearly state what is expected of the boy.

While expansively drunk, invite the boy to join him, treating the boy like a valued peer, perhaps even offering the boy a drink.

While drunk, violently curse at the boy, citing his behavior as evidence that he never has been and never will be any good. Perhaps the father will blame the mother for the boy's lack of character. Possibly he will be physically violent.

While morosely drunk, engage the boy in a monologue concerning the father's problems, perhaps including abuse of the mother and the boy.

While drunk, ignore the boy's homecoming.

While sober, ignore the boy's homecoming, feeling guilty at his own failures as a parent.

While either drunk or sober, abuse the mother, in the boy's presence, for the boy's misbehavior.

Come in later than the boy, thus avoiding the issue.

It is not hard to imagine one father going through all of the above, plus several other behaviors not stated, over a period of time. The probable effect of even a few of the above on the behavior of an adolescent who needs structure and limits is easily predicted.

The effect of drunkenness on decision making is similarly easy to predict. Again, although any particular decision the father makes may be fine, even inspired in its wisdom, the lack of consistency will make it impossible to depend on him. It is as if we know that a mechanic fails to tighten the wheel bolts only 10 percent of the time: we are still forced to check and retighten them 100 percent of the time or face disaster.

The father's maintenance function also suffers. Again, he may do a fine job some of the time, but it is hard to feel secure as he does electrical, plumbing, or other repair work. Better to call someone in, either to do it or to check Dad's work.

It is also hard to count on Dad as a spokesman for the family in conflict. Every interaction acquires the aspect of a game of Russian roulette. The odds may be numerically favorable, but one can emphatically lose.

In the affective area—the arena of feelings—drunkenness takes its biggest toll. Paul Watzlawick makes the point in *Pragmatics of Human Communication* that we cannot *not* communicate. To a family member the father's drunkenness looks as if he voluntarily acquired a debilitating disease which strikes and recedes at his will. The drunkenness itself is an eloquent communication, regardless of any drunken content. The drunkenness communicates to family members that they are held in less esteem than the bottle. The fact of drunkenness, with its accompanying pattern of self-deceit, lies, promises, and rationalizations, causes family members to discount all conscious communication. Imagine, for example, if a person you cared for said while drunk that he loved you more than anyone in the world. How would you feel? If drunkenness becomes a pattern, no one can believe anything that is said, at any time—drunk or sober.

Thus a pattern of fairly regular disabling drunkenness effectively cancels the father's function as a disciplinarian, decision maker, repairman, negotiator, and even as a communicating family member capable of giving or receiving love, support, or limits.

Faced with the fact that the father's function cannot be relied upon and that those functions are vital to the family's survival, the family finds itself consciously or unconsciously facing three unattractive alternatives:

1. Jettison the drunken father and try to reconstruct a functional family with the surviving members.

2. Stop functioning. If there is a simultaneous loss of functioning in more than one member, with the resulting physical and emotional drain on the remaining resources, the family could become what is known as a multiproblem, disorganized family. This means that the family abandons its function of providing life support and socialization for its membership. It drops rules and roles and becomes a group of biologically related persons coexisting on a survival level without structure or cooperation. This happens, but it tends to happen in culturally isolated families whose members cannot make contact with resources outside the family or who have no structure in which they believe.

3. Make adjustments to the new situation in an attempt to somehow keep going as a family with the same membership.

If the family were to meet and analyze the situation, carefully considering the options and their short- and long-term implications, it is quite possible that opinion number one (the exclusion of father) would emerge as the reluctant but preferred decision, but rarely is this the process. It is extremely difficult for a family to exclude a member and even more difficult when that member is a drunken father. The mother must feel strong enough to survive the loss and secure enough in her convictions to submit everyone else to loss and pain. As we shall see, this is very unlikely. In fact, although I can cite no statistics to support such a claim, I would guess that a family with an actively drinking male alcoholic can be more stable than a family without one. The low self-esteem of its members makes them extremely defensive and resistant to changes. Because option number two (stop functioning) is not an option but the result of the failure of options, the remaining option is the most likely. The family will attempt to remain intact and to keep functioning, a largely unrewarding task.

Crisis and Emergency

In part, option number three seems so inevitable because the family seldom becomes aware of the choice until long after it is made. In order to explain this, we must define a widely misunderstood term: crisis. A crisis is an event that confronts a system in an area where the system has no existing tools to cope. As a result, the system must recognize that the situation exists *and* must change to accommodate the new demands. This change may be either to dissolve, to learn new skills, or to adopt new structure, but remaining the same is *not* an option. Crisis *must* result in change.

Alcoholic families are often said to be crisis-oriented. This is an error. Alcoholic families are *emergency*-oriented. An emergency is a situation confronting a system which causes several of its members to become agitated. There is usually a plethora of loud noises and sudden, convulsive movements, followed by a return to the preexisting situation. An emergency can be distinguished from a crisis by the fact that systemic change does not follow an emergency.

If, for example, a family is gathered for breakfast and Father suddenly slumps over the table with a heart attack, the family is in crisis. The family is suddenly faced with the task of functioning without a key member. It has had no time or opportunity to learn tools with which to cope with the problem, so it is safe to predict that the family will stop functioning in its old way and (it is hoped) will learn new ways of functioning appropriate to its new situation.

The usual progress of alcoholism, however, slowly erodes the functioning of the father at a pace which allows the family time to develop tools for coping with the father's change in functioning. As Dad's behavior becomes less predictable, the family, either consciously or not, develops alternate plans to prepare for father's possible incapacity in key situations. These subtle adjustments allow the family to avoid crisis, reducing the impact of the father's radically decreased functioning to that of a series of emergencies. If the family does not have the capacity to make the necessary adjustments, it will, of course, fall apart. However, if it does have sufficient resources, it will adjust in ways that are predictable.

As the father's functioning becomes less consistent, responsibility to pick up the slack almost always falls on the coparent, the mother. Anyone who has tried to perform the mother role in a family knows it to be a full-time job. It would seem initially that father's incapacity would eventually impose most of another full-time job on her, but as we shall see, that is not exactly the case. We also have to account for the work imposed by alcoholism itself.

The task of discipline, for example, is hard enough to combine with the nurturing mother role, as any single mother (or father, for that matter) will attest. But disciplining children with active sabotage going on is doubly tricky. If a mother is scolding a son for coming in late, and her drunken husband tells her not to be so bitchy and to "let the kid have a little fun," she may find her message and authority seriously diluted, thus making the job of discipline less easily accomplished and more time and energy consuming.

Decision making also acquires new facets in an alcoholic household. Many more decisions need to be made: there are constant emergencies during which things must be decided, and contingency plans accounting for various states of drunkenness and intractability must be made for each family event. It is also hard to implement the decisions that have been made, and a great deal of time must be allotted to concealing decisions from the alcoholic or arguing about the ones which could not be concealed.

The task of negotiating with systems outside the family also becomes more complicated. There is the task of trying to explain negotiations attempted by Father, plus the fact that there seems to be much more negotiating necessary when there is an alcoholic in the home: bosses, doctors, creditors, victims—all must be reckoned with. It is time-consuming and frustrating work. The task of home maintenance tends to expand radically if there is an alcoholic in the home—especially if he attempts maintenance or repairs himself.

The affective function, however, is the one that suffers most. And unlike the other functions, this one is extremely difficult for the mother or anyone else to compensate by undertaking the role. The loss of a father's affective function is damaging over time in any family. When a family loses a father through death or divorce his emotional presence may not be the first thing missed—the loss of more concrete functions may be more immediately noticeable—but later on the loss of emotional presence is likely to have the most profound effect. When an alcoholic's emotional presence—in the sense of it being a resource—is lost to his family, he can no longer give love or support in a way his family can use. He does, at the same time have a profound negative emotional impact, spreading insecurity, fear, hate, guilt, and anger as a farmer spreads seeds. The mother then tries to take responsibility for these bad feelings and spends time and energy in the futile task of undoing them—time and energy which is at a premium.

It is clear then that as a father begins to drink dysfunctionally, the mother's function must alter itself to compensate for his decay. Her job changes from one that is already demanding to something very different, requiring highly specialized skills and characteristics.

The Co-Alcoholic

If we were perusing résumés in search of a person to fill this job, we would be well advised to catalog those qualities that are absolutely *necessary* in a serious candidate. When this question was submitted to workshop participants, the list of characteristics included:

1. High-level organizational ability.
2. Competence at a wide variety of tasks and the ability to learn additional ones quickly.
3. Stability and resistance to panic.
4. Skill at diplomacy and emotional manipulation.
5. Resilience with a high tolerance to pain.
6. High energy, with good resistance to fatigue.
7. Good administrative skills.
8. The ability to defer gratification indefinitely.
9. Crisis intervention skills.
10. Strong sense of morality. A sense of right and wrong is crucial in this person's thinking.
11. Loyalty and a willingness to put the needs of an important group before her own. It therefore helps if she is out of touch with her own needs and feelings.
12. Capacity to never ask "What's in this for *me?*"
13. The ability to do enormous amounts of work for a minimal payoff.
14. High level of nursing and caretaking skills.
15. Tendency toward overachievement leading to the ability to work consistently at 120 percent of capacity.
16. Gives low priority to her sexual needs and feelings. This is a subcategory of number twelve, but it calls for some special comment. Imagine a woman in this position who considered her sexuality to be important. If she focused these needs on her husband, it would make her emotion- ally vulnerable to a highly undependable person with whom she was in a power struggle and for whom she had contempt. Most alcoholics become less alluring as

sexual partners over time and usually incompetent as well. If the woman looked outside her marriage to meet these needs, she would have to direct a major amount of energy away from a family that was already suffering from an energy crisis. Her loyalty, task orientation, and moral structure would not permit this. If one is faced with a situation where a strong need cannot be gratified, the best strategy to avoid painful frustration is to direct one's attention away from that need and to define it as unimportant. A person who is hungry when no food is available does well to think about other things.

17. Is symptomatic. To be considered a symptom, a behavior must have two elements: It must control the context in which interaction takes place; and it must contain overtly or covertly the statement "I can't help it." Because drunkenness is such a powerful symptom, surviving while in constant contact with an alcoholic depends on having a "counter symptom." The necessary effect of the counter symptom is to defend the wife's boundaries without initiating dangerous conflict (more on this later). Symptoms such as migraine headaches, obesity, depression, and obsessive-compulsive behaviors are common among wives of alcoholics. If these are not present, some other symptom will be, because a tool to defend essential boundaries indirectly is absolutely essential for a person in this situation. The fact that such a woman necessarily has very strong feelings which must be repressed and suppressed can account for her symptoms psychodynamically.

18. Has low self-esteem with a very dependent personality framework. This is self-explanatory; this woman is a person who lives for others, needs others to live for. It is not likely that a person with high self-esteem would put up with a fraction of what an alcoholic's wife routinely tolerates.

The above characteristics describe a precise person and with a fairly high level of differentiation. It may therefore seem somewhat arrogant and irresponsible to claim, as I do, that all wives of alcoholics in functioning families who have been at the job for at least five years will possess *all* of the traits listed above. There will, of course, be variations according to native ability, cultural background, economic resources, aesthetics, and other factors, but any long-term female co-alcoholic will fit the pattern. This is only surprising until one realizes how demanding the job is and how few options it allows. It would, for example, be easy to list a highly differentiated set of traits describing a vice-president in charge of sales for a major corporation. When a job is sufficiently demanding, it will describe the person who holds it.

The Daughter as Apprentice

As can be seen, the co-alcoholic is a superachiever, but the demands of the job are such that even superwoman needs an assistant. Obviously the assistant must be recruited from the children, but which one will it be? Our hypothetical family has a son sixteen, a daughter fourteen, a son twelve, and a daughter ten. Of this group, one might imagine that the obvious choice for mother's assistant would be the older son. Upon reflection, however, it becomes clear why this almost never happens.

Although the older children in this family are adolescents, the recruiting of an assistant took place some years earlier, when the older children were in latency. The latency period is characteristically a period during which a child's energy is focused on acquiring the skills appropriate to being a man or a woman. Children of this age tend to play in sexually segregated groups in which sexual chauvinism is much in evidence. As the child attempts to learn how to be a man or woman, the primary model tends to be the same-sexed parent, as this is usually the adult the child has the best opportunity to observe in process over a period of time.

It is safe to assume, therefore, that a son will evidence many stylistic similarities to his father. In a family where the father is an irresponsible alcoholic, it is understandable that these similarities will be viewed with alarm by the mother. It will be difficult for her to assign responsibility to the son, and if out of fairness or desperation she does experiment with using him as a resource, her expectations probably will make the success of the experiment less likely.

Another factor conspires to make the selection of the son less likely. The duties most easily delegated to a child are jobs like child care and housework. Even in these days of more fluid sexual roles, jobs like this tend to be defined as "woman's work," and it therefore would take far more effort to convince a latency-age boy than girl to accept them. In a family where effort and energy are at a premium, this is a significant factor.

The older daughter, then, is the most likely recruit for mother's assistant. If a family has no daughters, a son must suffice. If there are several daughters fairly close in age, the oldest might not be the chosen one. If the drinking gets out of hand when the oldest daughter is already adolescent, for example, a younger girl, still in latency, is likely to get the call. But there is no question that the role must be played by someone if the family is to continue functioning. In my experience the only cases where this role was not played by a child according to the pattern described above was when the family possessed the financial resources to hire a surrogate on a cash basis. The fact that the family *must* fill this role to survive will be important when we discuss clinical strategies.

The training for the role of the mother's assistant is subtle and exacting. On the most basic level the child is taught that a good person looks for needs outside herself which must be met and de-emphasizes her awareness and value for internal needs. Traditional sex-role sterotypes are a powerful ally in this training, helping the girl learn that affiliation and service are the proper goals for a young woman.

The training of the young assistant co-alcoholic differs from that of her peers, in that she is taught that the primary tool for affiliation is service, not sexiness. Sexiness is no more job-appropriate for her than it is for her mother, and for some of the same reasons. A teenager who is involved with boyfriends and sexual politics cannot devote as much energy to what the family demands as her primary job. Moreover, because generational, personal, and behavioral boundaries tend not to be clearly defined in many alcoholic families, sexiness on the part of an adolescent girl is a risky stance, not only for the girl herself but for her mother as well.

Characteristically the relationship between the mother and her assistant is tense. This is not surprising when one remembers that nearly every adolescent girl has a tense relationship with her mother. In the alcoholic family, however, the natural separating and differentiating process is hampered by the structural necessity that forces the two females into very similar roles. A popular adolescent strategy for differentiating from the mother is to focus attention and energy outside the family, toward peers and outspokenly adolescent activities. This strategy is not available to a girl who must invest much of her energy on her family by performing an adult role. One frequent alternative for the girl is to ally with her father in his ongoing war against her mother. In most cases this merely consists of blaming her mother for her father's drinking and defending him against mother's *polemics*. Because the couple boundary in alcoholic families is typically weak, there is the danger that the mother will perceive this alliance as a threat to her marriage. Although the moral orientation and duty-bound programming of the daughter in the mother's assistant role makes her a much less likely candidate for incest than her sister (or sisters) might be, the uncertain boundaries still make the father-daughter alliance extremely anxiety provoking for all concerned. If the assistant de-emphasizes her sexuality, the situation can be alleviated.

Given these factors, coupled with a lack of experience, the daughter playing this role in the alcoholic family tends to move into the mating arena rather late, and when she does, it will be hard for her to place a high value on herself. She has been trained to distance herself from her sexuality, to think of her needs and opinions as unimportant, and to not expect affection or appreciation. The alcoholic family is not an effective self-esteem factory.

This daughter does, however, possess valuable features that she can offer to a potential mate: loyalty, unselfishness, administrative and nursing skills, as well as a willingness to assume any responsibility she may feel needs to be taken on. When she marries, it is also likely that she is gainfully employed at a steady, responsible, if not especially remunerative job. Need we ask what job that is? When this question is presented at training groups, the correct answers flow immediately: she is, of course, a nurse. She may also be a day-care teacher or a teacher of the handicapped, a hospital attendant, a social worker, or an alcoholism counselor. But nursing—apart from being specifically accurate—is an excellent metaphor for her vocational framework. It is a job that involves caring for the young or infirm and damaged in a very intimate manner. The nurse has almost unlimited responsibility for this care but little direct authority for it—that is given to the doctor. The doctor enjoys more freedom and power than the nurse, is much better rewarded, and is held in greater esteem by society, although the nurse can make a strong case that her position requires as much dedication, hard work, and moral integrity.

We can even predict what kind of nurse this young woman will be. She will be a marvelous nurse, conscientious, responsible, technically competent, and dedicated. She will have some difficulty treating patients in a truly respectful manner ("Did we drink our juice this morning?"), but will always be courteous and proper. She will have few friends but will have responsible working relationships with her coworkers. If extra responsibility must be scheduled, she will accept it and discharge it well. Eventually, of course, such a nurse will be promoted to supervisor, where she will be a disaster.

This may seem strange until one realizes that there is one skill that can never be acquired in an alcoholic family: a capacity for trusting others to keep promises, carry out commitments, or tell the truth. A person learning to trust others in an alcoholic family is as likely as a child learning Turkish in a family that speaks only English. Neither parent keeps his or her word: The father has promised to control his drinking and to be more responsible 488,391 times to date, while the mother has said things like "I really need you to babysit this Friday night—you can go out next Friday night." Next Friday, of course, the mother needs her "one more time."

Therefore this young woman has never seen responsibility effectively delegated, accepted, and carried out. As an administrator she has trouble trusting that a task she assigns will be successfully carried out. She therefore checks closely and oversupervises, not out of meanness or malice, but because she *knows* at a very deep level that the only way things are going to be done right is if she controls the process—and she is responsible for seeing that things are done right. She does not accept responsibility lightly.

Accordingly, as she assigns a task and then gives the person assigned a clear message that she doesn't believe she is competent to carry it out, the person assigned is forced to choose between two alternatives: either to accept the attribution of incompetence and become passive and dependent, or to rebel, either directly or passive-aggressively. Thus, the daughter-turned-supervisor will have either a depressed, dependent staff or a rebellious and passive-aggressive staff. If you have been in a hospital recently, your experience may now seem more understandable.

In the daughter's personal life, many of the same dynamics take place. There is considerable evidence that suggest that the most important influences on a person's behavior are the expectations of the important people around them. Robert Rosenthal, in *Pygmalion in the Classroom,* has done several fascinating, if ethically questionable studies in which he switched the records of the students in a junior high school that used the tracking system. The tracking system divides students into separate programs depending on some indicators of academic ability. Characteristically, the A track goes to college, the B track goes to work, and the C track goes to jail. In a new and large junior high school where the teachers and students did not know each other, teachers who were to teach an A track class were given records of B track students with only the names changed. The teachers were told something like "These are good kids. If you don't push them too hard or get too demanding they will be happy and get a lot out of the course."

Teachers who were getting a B track class were told, "You better stay on your toes. These kids are always asking questions and doing special projects. If you don't know your stuff now, you will by the end of the year. Don't try to stay just one chapter ahead of these kids." Here, too, the records were switched. In both classes, the teachers did not know of the switch. Result: the A track students did B track work and vice versa.

Let's look at another illustration of this principle that expectations govern behavior. Suppose a man, for whatever hereditary and environmental reasons, develops a conviction that any woman with whom he has a relationship will sleep with any Tom, Dick, and Harry. This assumption could severely affect the behavior of any woman to whom he relates. Whether or not she has an inclination to be fickle, she will find herself constantly suspected and accused. Nearly everything she does or doesn't do will be interpreted as evidence of her promiscuity. Given a situation like this, the woman can respond in a number of ways. She can leave the relationship, change her name, and move to another state. This is by far the most effective response, and if she considers it open to her the problem is solved. If, however, leaving the relationship is not an option she will consider, she must convince her man of her loyalty and good behavior. There is little chance of success in this task, and the woman's failure will leave her continuing to try in spite of the apparent futility of her efforts. (This option merely delays the crunch.) She can also respond to the situation by blaming the man's distrust on herself and accepting his definition of her. If he is correct, then she is a woman of easy virtue and as such is open to promiscuous behavior. She may, however, avoid this pitfall only to fall into the third: Finally fed up with his constant accusations, she begins to look for a way to retaliate. What better way is there to punish him for his suspiciousness than to do what will *really* hurt him?

This is not to say that a woman accused of promiscuity will automatically render the accusation prophetic, but merely to give an example of how a person's expectations of a spouse can increase the probability that the feared behavior will occur.

But back to our older daughter. What then does the mother's assistant expect from men? From relationships? In short, men are irresponsible, uncaring, and prone to drink, and their women must care for them and manage their affairs without thanks or credit. This belief is not, as a rule, consciously held, any more than is the belief that a chair will hold your weight. We can infer that a person believes that a chair will hold weight if that person acts as if it were true (i.e., if he or she sits down without hesitation). Similarly, since the mother's assistant acts as if her man were irresponsible and needed care, we can guess that she believes that most men are like her father.

This assumption is reinforced by her assumptions about herself. As we noted, she has entered the courtship arena later than her contemporaries and has little sense of herself as valuable in her own right. She views her ability to manage and nurse, as well as her capacities for loyalty and unselfishness, as the most valuable attributes she could offer a potential mate. If she were to meet an independent man who wanted to control and administer his own life and who was seeking a self-fulfilled partner to share it with him, he would define as negative the very traits she valued in herself—hardly a promising start for a relationship. If, however, she takes up with a man who values a woman who can care for him and relieve him of life's boring details, romance has a far better chance to flourish!

Every service has its price. An unconscious corollary of taking care of another is believing that the person needs caretaking. The mother's assistant from an alcoholic family has no cognitive model for a man who is dependable or responsible: Therefore, her planning and actions will be based on the assumptions that he is neither. In addition, her skills for relating to men do not extend beyond rescuing and caretaking, so she needs to find someone who can use her services in order to feel valued herself.

Example: On his way to work her new mate spies a pile of envelopes containing payments for the month's bills. He pockets them, stating that he will mail them on the way to work. Since it is her job to see that things are done right, she will naturally ask him if he mailed them when he returns. But when he claims he has mailed them, will she check his pockets? My guess is that she must—the payments are important, and she has no experience that men do what they say.

The incident cited above is mundane, but it will be repeated in varied forms countless times.

Given the lack of trust in his competence—amplified by her considerable competence and moral righteousness—it is a rare man who can resist feeling secondary, powerless, and resentful, and as we know, there are medicines specific for these feelings. It may be that this young woman's new spouse has no particular dependence on alcohol, but given her past, there is no way for her to be indifferent to his drinking.

Example; They are in a restaurant. The waiter asks if they will have a cocktail. He orders one; she may even order one as well. Dinner is slow in coming. He orders another, she doesn't. Although she controls her reaction, a careful observer might notice a perceptible tightening at the corners of her mouth. When the husband orders a beer with dinner, however, it will require almost superhuman restraint on her part to avoid saying something like ''You've already had two drinks, are you sure you need a beer?''

As her husband feels less and less competent and effectual in relation to her, he will clearly be in the market for ways to feel powerful in this woman's presence. Confronting her is difficult because her moral position is likely to include a well-documented account of his inability to take responsibility, such as all the times he didn't keep promises or in some other significant way proved himself to be inadequate. It will be easy for her to demonstrate why she is forced to take responsibilities on herself, and he will find himself unable to fight her indictment. There is, however, one thing that really gets to her and simultaneously makes him feel powerful in the relationship. She can manage many things, but she can't manage his drinking. Just as it is more probable that the wife in the first example will become promiscuous, the husband of a mother's assistant is more likely to become alcoholic. There is a certain elegant symmetry here. An alcoholic can train an alcoholic's wife: a mother's assistant can also train an alcoholic. Of course, it is much easier if her husband has had previous training. This brings us to a profile of the older son.

Chronic Punk Syndrome:
The Older Son

The older son in this family provides a great deal of work for people in the human services and criminal justice fields. Although styles vary, his development is equally predictable. In grade school he tends to be quiet and withdrawn. He is a poor student but not spectacularly so. Because there are myriad problems and a dearth of energy and resources in school systems, he is unlikely to attract attention until he is in junior high. Around the onset of puberty his problems will escalate, usually in a passive manner. Truancy, a sharp decline in his already marginal academic functioning, a vigorous testing of parental rules (which will be found wanting)—all of these will prelude the arrival of the central theme: drugs.

Somewhere in early adolescence, certainly by age sixteen, this boy will discover drugs, and they will snap into his life as if the fit were milled by a skilled machinist. They will almost immediately become a central coping mechanism, he will begin to associate with similar punks, and he will get into trouble. The trouble will vary with the drugs and the social circumstances. He may get violent and addicted quickly or meander into a more leisurely pattern of academic failure, marginal, unsatisfactory employment, frustration, and a slow development of alcoholism, abetted, perhaps, by a relationship with a mother's assistant from another family.

Whether the trouble comes sooner or later—and regardless of whether this young man is passive or violent, affluent or poor—it will come, and it will involve drugs. Regardless of what drugs this boy starts with, he is likely to become partial to central nervous system depressants: opiates, barbiturates, and especially alcohol. This is so because these drugs act as a surrogate. Once he finds his drug, it is hard to predict what will happen but the drug is not likely to play a positive role in his life or the lives of those around him. Without intervention, he may die quickly and violently, become a professional convict, or become simply a mainstream alcoholic who for a period of time will appear to function in the family and on the job. The variations are infinite, but the theme is well defined.

As with all of the roles defined here, an intervention can render the situation less predictable and open new options. In the case of the chronic punk syndrome, the intervention must have three elements to be successful:

1. A clearly communicated and consistently enforced structure, such as a residential treatment program with explicit limits.
2. An opportunity for the boy to learn skills upon which he can base self-esteem.
3. An opportunity for him to learn certain basic interpersonal skills, principally boundary enforcement and negotiation ("Excuse me, you are standing on my foot. Would you please move?").

If these three elements are a consistent part of his environment for an extended period of time, there is a good chance that this boy (or girl) can stop depending on chemicals, learn to relate responsibly, and live a happy, productive life, perhaps as a drug or alcoholism counselor.

The Younger Children

As we discuss the younger children in this family, it should be understood that not all, or even most, younger children in alcoholic families will fit the following descriptions. In less-regressed families, in fact, the younger children can resemble the two types of young people already described. However, severe disturbance does occur in extremely deteriorated families in which the parenting functions have all but disappeared. The following descriptions are of children who have grown up in such a regressed, chaotic atmosphere, where most of the nurturing falls to resentful older siblings, where basic needs are not met, where violence and incest are constant possibilities, and where there is no consistency of experience or structure.

Unlike his older brother, the *younger son* is likely to attract professional attention quite early. He may have his first school core evaluation in kindergarten or the first grade. At this evaluation one will hear phrases such as "low impulse control," "learning disorder," "inadequate socialization and peer relations," or even "sociopath." The latter might seem a melodramatic term to apply to a boy likely to be no more than three feet high, but the person who has had the experience of being between this child and something he wants might not find the term so hyperbolic. This child will actively challenge any authority structure in which he finds himself, and it will be a rare structure that can meet the challenge. As he gets older, he, too, is likely to abuse drugs. His drug use will not be as central to his problem as it is to his older brother's, but it will be one feature of a discouraging terrain.

This boy is born to lose. There is no question that he will run afoul of the law. The only question will be when his first felony arrest will occur. One could safely bet before he enters high school. If he does enter high school, the odds against his graduation are astronomical. By the time his contemporaries are graduating, his education has been entrusted to the criminal justice system. As can be readily inferred, the clinical prognosis for this boy is poor and becomes more grim with every year of his life. Very structured, long-term residential programs with heavy behavior modification components have a chance if they get this boy when he is young enough, but few of these boys will have such programs available to them.

70 /   FAMILIES UNDER THE INFLUENCE

Family therapy might help the family create a viable situation for this boy if he is young enough. It is hard to imagine that any individual outpatient therapy would be adequate to the task.

In some alcoholic families, the *younger daughter* is a trainee for the mother's helper role. When this is the case she will, of course, develop some of the characteristics of her older sister, but may deviate significantly from the classic form. For example, she is far more likely to use drugs or other forms of acting out than her sister. By the time her training begins, the family is less organized, and the example of her older sister might give rise to doubts about the rewards of virtue. This child is likely to have many characteristics in common with the older son. Sex-role expectations are more likely to lead her into the mental health system rather than the criminal justice system, and with appropriate intervention (not dissimilar to what her brother needs) she has a good chance to get control of her life.

If, however, the family is more regressed in her early years, or a responsible role is not available to her for other reasons, we are likely to see another picture. This child is generally physically immature, underweight, and withdrawn. She will probably come to the attention of professionals shortly after she begins school, often because teachers will report that she makes little contact or exhibits some inappropriate affect or other behavior. Sometimes her evaluation will describe her as schizophrenic or having a ''schizo-affective'' disorder. If she can function in school she will be socially and academically marginal at best. She may become pregnant as soon as she has the biological capacity to do so. Even if she comes from a less-regressed family and does not exhibit the kind of severe physical and emotional failure to thrive described above, she is very prone to premature pregnancy.

An alcoholic family is a very difficult place for a girl (or boy) to develop a comfortable view of self and sexuality. The stabilizing roles of parent and child are not adhered to, with Father frequently forgoing his parental authority to receive caretaking from his children. This lack of generational boundaries, along with the presence of drunkenness and its concomitant loss of impulse control, makes incest a distinct possibility. Although the "parental" older daughter is less likely to be involved in this behavior for reasons already explained, clinicians should not assume that the child in the mother's helper role is immune from sexual abuse. The younger daughters are vulnerable enough to warrant investigating the possibility of sexual abuse in all alcoholic families.

The above is not a pleasant picture. People who are unfamiliar with alcoholic families are sometimes irritated by what must strike them as unsupported overgeneralization. Those who are familiar with such families are aware of the accuracy of the picture. It is depressing to realize the vast number of families that conform to this model, down to the smallest detail.

Once when I described this model to a group of alcoholic families who were participating in a hospital treatment program, there was a long pause after the alcoholic's wife was described as "In spite of everything, getting the kids off to school with a good breakfast, keeping an immaculate house, and active in civic organizations." Finally one woman raised her hand, rose, and said, "I was never active is civic organizations." The outburst of laughter that followed confirmed how the model matched experience. It is awesome how a drug can homogenize and organize very diverse people in such predictable patterns.

At this point it is important to note that while repeated drunkenness is sufficient to form the family structure described above, alcoholism does not have to be present for a family to achieve a nearly identical structure. Unfortunately, if the father is unable to be active, loving, and competent for whatever reason, the model may develop.

There are many implications growing out of this model that will not be treated here in depth, but which it seems useful to touch upon. The first is that traditional Judeo-Christian sex-role expectations greatly facilitate the development of this family structure. The paradigm of the nurturing, politically subservient mother (the "queen of the home") makes it hard for the wife to feel empowered to correct the process before it becomes chronic. Because women are taught that their status is based on that of the man with whom they affiliate, it is risky for a woman to call attention to the fact that her man is not functioning. She is encouraged by still-prevalent mores to see his drinking as her failure, which tempts her to ally with the denial process.

The role expectations for men also contribute to the development of alcoholic families. A man is not "expected" to provide affective support for his family. If he functions as a breadwinner, he is functioning adequately in his role by current standards. Drinking, even drunkenness, is often considered a prerogative of a hardworking man. Sometimes even mild (short of requiring hospitalization) physical abuse of spouse or children is included within this license. There is therefore some social support for highly destructive, pathological behavior. This is further reinforced by the "strong silent" ego ideal held out to men. The Marlboro Man image forbids vulnerability, expression of strong feeling (except murderous rage), or uncertainty. This man must "do it alone" and "fight his own battles." Not only does this image make a chemical antidote to powerless feelings very attractive, but it also makes recognition and treatment of a drinking problem that much harder.*

---

*It is noteworthy that the first step to recovery through the A.A. program is to accept that one cannot "fight" alcohol and that one needs the help of a "higher power" to survive—moves which deliberately counter this macho isolationist mindset. A brilliant examination of how A.A. is designed to combat this image can be found in Gregory Bateson's essay "The Cybernetics of 'Self': Toward a Theory of Alcoholism," in *Steps to an Ecology of Mind* (San Francisco: Chandler Publishing Co., 1972).

3

Treating
Alcoholic Families

The art of change is handicapped by much of its heritage from the medical model. Of all the medical traditions, few are as enervating as the notion that all diseases have prescribed treatments that follow from accurate diagnosis of the disease in the patient. A counselor or change agent knows that the most powerful determinant of treatment strategy is not the condition from which the patient is suffering, but the context in which one sees the patient. If a man is suffering from alcoholism, for example, and he presents himself for treatment because he is tired of himself and his drinking, the treatment strategy is radically different from the approach used if he comes to treatment because his boss told him he would be fired if he didn't. When diagnosis includes a careful assessment of the patient's context (family, work, and social categories), then prescribing successful interventions becomes possible.

Alcoholic families come into treatment in three basic categories of contexts. In each of these contexts the identified patient is different, and treatment strategies vary accordingly. The first major category is through the children. This may occur when the older son is arrested, say, for driving a vehicle without authorization while under the influence of alcohol and is sent to a court diversion program or a court clinic. The older daughter might go to the counseling service of her nursing school complaining of depression. The impetus might also be a core evaluation at the school or a pregnancy counseling session. In any case, one of the children in the family comes to the attention of a helping professional.

When this happens, a professional who has not been trained to see presenting problems in the context of the family in which it occurs often regards the problem as if it were a disease affecting the child alone, like measles. If the family is considered in the treatment, it is viewed as a "resistant" force in combat with the therapist. These notions are far from absurd and have a compelling logic: however, the conclusions one draws from this logic will lead one to choose too small a treatment unit to be effective. It is a good rule of thumb for the therapist to see as much of a family as possible when confronted by the problem of a dependent child or spouse. The therapist seeing a child from an alcoholic family will notice that the family will make moves to exclude the drinking parent from the treatment unit. If the father does come in, drinking will rarely be mentioned and will almost never be cited as a problem. Most often the available treatment unit will be the child and the mother. If this is the case, it is advisable to begin the treatment with this part of the family while continually looking for ways to get the rest of the family to join the therapy.

In the second context, the wife in the alcoholic family presents herself for treatment. Workers in mental health are so familiar with the initial interview that they sometimes find themselves answering questions while the client is asking them. The interview usually goes like this: the woman is thirty-five–forty-five years old, intelligent and neatly dressed. She appears depressed, and her voice carries a strong undertone of annoyance. She is likely to be overweight or even obese. Her litany of woe includes conflict, public humiliation, sometimes violence, and serious problems with the children, collection agencies, illness, and—most of all—drunkenness. The drunkenness may be laid right out, or it may need to be coaxed out of her by skillful interviewing, but it will emerge as the cause of all of the aforementioned troubles. Things seem pretty straight-forward until the interviewer asks how long the situation has been going on. The reply is invariably something like "twenty-one years."

How, the interviewer will speculate, has this apparently sane and intelligent woman put up with an intolerable situation for so long? And why did she come in today?

The answer to the first question has been alluded to in our discussion of the personality traits of the alcoholic's wife: her loyalty, "unselfishness," dependency, and scripting as a self-sacrificing nurse-caretaker made the option of leaving the alcoholic spouse unthinkable to this woman. The answer to the second question—What brings her in today?—is always the same: Her husband has broken a rule.

The rules, of course, vary from household to household. In some families it goes "You can drink all you want, but never let me catch you with another woman." In others it may be "You can drink and run around with other women all you want, but keep your hands off me and the kids," or even "You can drink, run around, and beat us all you want, but bring home a paycheck every Friday."

Whatever the rules are, the fact that this woman is in the clinic is evidence that one has been broken. Because this kind of client is so frequently seen, one would think that counselors would have a clear idea of how to help her. Unfortunately this is not true. In fact this woman is one of the most difficult types of clients—and with good reason.

The fact that she is much more mindful of the needs of others than she is of her own means that she quickly becomes aware of her counselor's need to feel helpful and effective. She is therefore likely to stay in treatment for a long time, telling the counselor how helpful the counseling is while making no changes whatsoever. Indeed, her great stability makes any kind of change slow and difficult for her. Another complicating factor is the fact that the woman's constant bitter complaints about her husband's drinking lead the counselor to believe that she wishes it to stop. Nothing could be farther from the truth. Like anyone else who has experienced a major change in her life (the breaking of the rule), she wants to return to her old world (in which her husband drank and followed the rules).

In most cases the counseling settles down to a predictably ineffective pattern in which the client tries to make the changes she knows she should make but fails. In some cases the counselor's impatience coupled with the client's guilt combine to precipitate some radical change, such as delivering an ultimatum to the husband and moving out of the house. But such changes invariably lead to disaster, since the client is completely unprepared to deal with the impact of her precipitous move. The counselor is faced with the dilemma of working with someone who is extremely slow to change, but who lives in an intolerable situation in which serious emergency follows serious emergency. This is a person who is not aware of her feelings and does not own her needs. When she finally acknowledges her feelings, she feels angry, hopeless, and justifiably afraid. Furthermore she is a dutiful, hardworking person who wants to do the right thing, and at last, in spite of her fears, she follows her counselor's advice—and then falls apart. Finally the counselor feels equally hopeless, inadequate, and depressed.

The third context in which the alcoholic family comes into treatment is during a period of genuine crisis when, for example, the alcoholic stops drinking. In this case the counselor is likely to have access to the alcoholic rather than other family members. This context offers the best opportunity for quick positive change, but there are traps nonetheless.

The first is to see the alcoholic's abstinence as the goal of treatment rather than a condition which allows treatment to begin. The inexperienced counselor is likely to see the family as recipients of a boon rather than as people whose lives have fallen apart and who need more help than the abstaining alcoholic.

It is hard to know why someone quits drinking. An A.A. member will say he "hit bottom," but it is hard to understand why one man's "bottom" is another's minor inconvenience. Stories abound of alcoholics who have lost jobs, families, and health, who resisted imprecations from friends, family, clergy, and physician, and who one day broke a shoelace and never took another drink. In any case if an alcoholic has a family and he quits drinking, the family is in crisis. All of its coping strategies suddenly become irrelevant to their life situation, and the anxiety levels of its members shoot off the measurable scale.

Consider, for example, the wife who for the past fifteen years got down each day on her knees and prayed that her husband would stop drinking. Now he has, and she is more miserable than before. Her misery is compounded and complicated by the fact that she is a highly moral person and there is no way in her framework for her to feel bad about her husband's sobriety and still be a good person. Therefore her bad feelings are feelings no one should have; they cannot be admitted. It is also difficult for her to feel good about her husband's abstinence: her whole life has been organized around his unpredictable irresponsibility, and now he is becoming "responsible." All her skills have been developed to deal with his drunkenness, and she has none to deal with him sober. Suddenly her life is rendered unmanageable by someone who is being praised for his new behavior. The same people are telling her how lucky she is, and she has no way of admitting that instead of feeling lucky—as she should—she feels resentful, frightened, and guilty.

A common reaction to this frightening situation is to ignore it and try to pretend that it is wonderful. The woman forces her face into an unconvincing smile and talks about how great everything is. There is nothing great about the choices that face her: She can change most of her behavior and emotional patterns, she can go crazy, or she can get her husband to go back to drinking. These will be discussed in reverse order.

It is a characteristic of any system that it will act to negate change in its environment or structure. This characteristic, called homeostasis, expresses itself with infinite variety. It is useful to think of the alcoholic behaviors under discussion as expressions of a system rather than as acts caused by the motivations of an individual. It is not that the wife wants her husband to drink again, it is just that the system moves to return to its "normal" state of functioning. Accusing family members of "trying" to get the alcoholic to drink again will bring heartfelt and valid denials. The members of the system are simply acting in understandable ways to cope with what confronts them. A counselor who tries to protect the sobriety of the alcoholic by fighting his family will do no good for anyone. Some of the common patterns through which homeostasis can express itself are outlined below.

Plan A: Anyone who has tried to express anger (or any emotion) to a person who is drunk quickly realizes the futility of trying to communicate. Living with an alcoholic thus creates a vast reservoir of unexpressed anger. Now that the husband is not drinking and cannot hide himself behind drunkenness, his wife would like to tell him the things she has had to put up with in the past. Because she is loyal and has tried to be fair, only the most documented and outrageous transgressions are included. Upon hearing these he, quite appropriately, feels worthless, ashamed, and powerless. There is, of course a specific drug that will cure these feelings.

Plan B: Wife says to husband, "I'm so glad you are taking such an interest in the children since you stopped drinking. I'm worried about Bruno, he's been staying out late and coming home drunk. Could you talk to him?"

Dutifully our newly sober friend waits up to confront Bruno, who, sure enough, shows up late and drunk. He lays down the law, to which Bruno replies, "*You're* talking to *me* about drinking?" and laughs his way up the stairs. How does our hero feel? What can he do about those feelings?

Plan C: Because everyone in the family is now under stress, members might start to express their stress symptomatically, according to their own styles. For example, Mom gets so depressed she can't function, the older son gets arrested, the older daughter drops out of school and comes home to help the younger son, and the younger daughter gets pregnant. Lucky for them there is a tower of strength in the family who feels responsible enough to straighten the whole thing out. How do you think he will do? How will he feel about that? What will he do then?

These examples show how a system's normal response to an internal or external change often negates that change. There could be a Plan D, E, and so on. While it is hard to anticipate what form the sabotage will take, the therapist should be pre- pared for the system to act against the abstinence and be ready to recognize the response for what it is.

Strategic Goals for Therapy

Although the problems are serious and the odds seem stacked against change, there are clear and effective strategies for working with alcoholic families that proceed logically from certain basic premises. Because some of these premises are radically different from those underlying traditional psychother- apy, they may seem jarring to readers until the pattern emerges.

The counselor's job is to make changes happen. This is dif- ferent from waiting until the client is "ready for change" or has "hit bottom." If the counselor is not able to initiate the changes that are held up as goals, the counselor has failed and must find new tactics to meet the goals. If the goals are met and the family still is not satisfying the needs of its members, the basic strategies must be amended.

When dealing with alcoholic families, it is important to understand that they are suffering from a condition that is not only dangerous to their own physical and emotional well-being, but that of others. They are teaching their children patterns that may be taken up by following generations. It is important that the counselor feel responsible to intervene whether or not any or all of the family members "seek help." Members of alco- holic families are ambivalent about most things, like all the rest of their human brothers and sisters. Every alcoholic wants to stop drinking and every recovering alcoholic wishes he or she could start drinking again. That goes for their spouses and children. Given the conflicting forces at work in an alcoholic family, ambivalence is an understandable condition and one that becomes significant only when we think about the ethics of intervention with a system that is inherently destructive. Typically, mental health workers are taught to respect a client's right to refuse treatment regardless of how obvious the need for treatment may be. But when one tries to translate these arguments to systems in which drunken driving, battering and sexual abuse, child neglect, and economic parasitism are the rule rather than an aberration, and in which these patterns will follow down the generations, the arguments for "respecting the client's choice" lose their academic objectivity as well as their relevance. Alcoholic families will *never* be unambivalently engaged in therapy, and waiting for them to "resolve their ambivalence" will only cause more professionals to claim that alcoholics are too resistant for treatment.

The goals a therapist will work toward when treating the alcoholic family are:

1. Stop the drinking, or if this is not possible, isolate the drinking member, lessening his/her impact on the other members (this is *much* less preferable).
2. Stop behavior that threatens the lives, health, or freedom of family members or others; this includes criminal activity and psychiatric symptoms, as well as behavior that facilitates destructive behavior in other family members.
3. Move children out of parental roles and sabotage inappropriate child-parent alliances.
4. Once the drinking is no longer an issue, help the parental alliance re-form so that parental authority will be effective.
5. Assist whichever family members are in need of help or support them to obtain appropriate resources outside the family (A.A., Al-Anon, Alateen, counseling, women's consciousness-raising groups, sex therapy, and so forth).

There are general strategic goals which will be appropriate for most alcoholic families, regardless of which members are available to the therapist or how the family came to be in treatment. Almost everyone in human services would agree with these goals. Some may add others, some would object to non–A.A.–oriented support, but in general there is nothing controversial, original, or exciting about this list. The interest lies in the tactics that serve to accomplish these goals. But first, a look at what usually happens when an alcoholic walks into a mental health center.

Common Pitfalls
in Working with Alcoholics

As mentioned earlier, traditional psychiatry has failed to devise even moderately successful treatment approaches for alcoholics. Many groups of patients who are not helped by psychiatry continue to show up for their hour, suffering with dignity, but their lack of progress goes unnoticed. However, when you are unsuccessful with an alcoholic, you know it, as does everyone else. The symptoms of alcoholism can be recognized without advanced training, so that it is not hard to see when the patient is getting nowhere in treatment. Not only do they not get better, but alcoholics also have a way of making people who try to help them feel awful. They seem to have an uncanny ability to perceive the parts of a helper's personality with which he or she is not comfortable and to keep directing attention to that area. Because alcoholics expect rejection and disapproval they are usually quite successful at training helpers to disapprove of them and reject them. One of the most common ways they do this is through a pattern identified by Eric Berne as the Rescue Triangle in his book *Games People Play*.

The Rescue Triangle is a game that requires at least two players: (1) The Victim, a person who cannot function successfully and seeks help, and (2) The Rescuer, a person who needs to help people, a perfect counterpart for the help-seeking victim.

Move 1 / V The Victim, in a state of disrepair, goes to the

Rescuer for help. The Victim usually cites the unsuccessful efforts of others to help, willingly accepting the blame for these failures. Move 1 / R The Rescuer follows good counseling practices, listening actively, remaining steadfastly nonjudgmental, holding the Victim in unconditional positive regard as much as possible. Perhaps the Rescuer offers some helpful insights. It is of course important for the Rescuer to disassociate with previous unsuccessful helpers so that the Victim can hope that this time will be different.

Move 2 / V The Victim, after initial reticence, warms to the Rescuer, laughs at the Rescuer's jokes, and perhaps sharing some painful personal material, even says with amazement, "I never told anyone that before!" Before leaving, the Victim makes another appointment.

Move 2 / R The Rescuer feels good about what happened and is cautiously optimistic. The Rescuer is somewhat skeptical that the Victim will show up for the appointment.

Move 3 / V The Victim shows up early for the appointment. Brief initial reticence is followed by warm acceptance. He makes statements like "You sure see through me! Nobody ever understood me like that before!" The Victim also reports progress with the problem. If it is alcoholism, then perhaps the Victim has attended an A.A. meeting and found it "all right," and promises, without enthusiasm, to attend another, "If you think it will help."

Move 3 / R The Rescuer is more optimistic. The relationship is clearly therapeutic. There is a long way to go, but progress is being made.

Move 4 / V The Victim shows up looking much better, glint in his eye, spring in his step. He is warm, respectful, and grateful to the counselor. More progress. Going to A.A. meeting has "cut my drinking way down." The Victim talks about how terrible things were before counseling.

Move 4 / R Rescuer is happy with the progress. Some things the Victim is saying are difficult to accept, however. Cutting down on drinking, for instance, is not going to help an alcoholic, but will make it much harder to accept the fact of alcoholism. The Rescuer chooses not to confront this because the confrontation would endanger an obviously helpful and therapeutic relationship. This is called the Patsy position.

Move 5 / V The Victim calls the Rescuer at three A.M. from a police station or detoxification unit. The Victim is drunk and apologetic. "I guess I let you down."

Move 5 / R The Rescuer is furious. Hard work and high hopes are dashed. He or she may clearly express the anger or try to mask it behind "professional objectivity." This is called the Persecutor position.

Move 6 / V The Victim realizes that the Rescuer is "just like everyone else" and never "really cared" about the Victim. The Victim feels abandoned and rejected. There is now no reason not to continue to kill himself. After all, nobody cares.

Move 6 / R The Rescuer feels guilty about getting angry and persecuting the Victim. He or she begins a self-persecution about setting impossible standards, getting overinvolved, and overreacting. A psychoanalytically oriented Rescuer will talk about countertransference and resolve to be more objective with the next client.

Move 7 / V The Victim again walks into Rescuer's office, feeling guilty and repentant.

Move 7 / R The Rescuer listens sympathetically, while vowing not to be taken in again. And off we go again. If this pattern continues for a year or more it is called "long-term psychotherapy." If the Rescuer charges enough and insists on seeing the client several times a week, it is called "psychoanalysis."

This pattern is called the "Rescue Triangle" because it can be diagrammed thus:

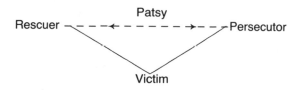

Notice that the Rescuer does all the moving, while the Victim remains stationary. While the only way for therapists to insure that they will never rescue is not to care about their clients, there are definite tools, tactics, and concepts that can provide some protection from the Rescue pattern and help a therapist recognize and correct it more quickly.

In helping relationships it is always difficult to know with any degree of exactness what responsibility the client must take and what must be done by the therapist. In the above scenario, the counselor (heretofore known as the Rescuer) attempted to help the alcoholic with the tools that training had provided. As we saw, these proved to be inadequate, despite the counseler's honorable intentions. The methods for treating alcoholic families that will be presented make it possible to get out of the Rescue Triangle and actually assist alcoholics and their families to change. However, before going into treatment interventions, we should review some of the central theoretical assumptions that underlie the treatment strategies. This leads first to a discussion of interpersonal power and then to a look at how symptoms function within a system.*

Power: The Dynamics
of Personal Interaction

The importance of the concept of power in understanding drunkenness was spelled out earlier. It would follow that a counselor working with systems where drunkenness is a common occurrence had better understand something about power and how it operates in relationships. Unfortunately, training programs for counselors, social workers, substance abuse workers, psychologists, and medical personnel often omit the teaching of interpersonal politics. This leaves the helper with

---

*The following sections draw heavily on the work of Paul Watzlawick, Janet Beavin Bavelas, and Don D. Jackson *(Pragmatics of Human Communication)* and on the work of Jay Haley *(Strategies of Psychotherapy)*.

few conscious tools to combat the unconscious power maneuvers of his clientele.

Interpersonal power can be defined as the ability to control the context in which behavior takes place. The person who controls the context sets the tone and creates the framework through which an interaction will be viewed. There are four basic *power relationships* possible between any two people:* the first is

Symmetry   I'm Boss   I'm Boss

Ⓐ──⟶   ⟵──Ⓑ

Symmetry in a power relationship is a state that exists between two people when they are both doing the same thing: attempting to control the context. It is a state of open power conflict. A will move to define the context and B will oppose A's definition or make a counterdefinition. For example, if A and B are a couple about to go out on a date, A might say, "Let's go to the movies." B might say, "Let's go dancing." A: "Movies." B: "Dancing." A: "Movies." B: "Dancing." And so on—and on.

Movies   Dancing

Ⓐ──⟶   ⟵──Ⓑ

If this process continues, midnight will arrive with A and B still at home, each with hot little knots in their stomachs. They have not gone to the movies, they have not gone dancing, but they have expended several times more energy than if they had done both. At this point they might be curious as to their other options, which seem to be: (1) Get married. Everyone knows such a couple. They fight about everything. Any move made by one is opposed by the other—and off they go. Many people are mystified by the fact that these people have remained together

---

*Watzlawick et al., *Pragmatics of Human Communication*.

while other more amiable couples are on their second divorce. These are people who are lucky—or unlucky—enough to find another person with a similar style of distance regulation. While fighting they remain in contact (a human need) while avoiding intimacy (frightening for most people, in spite of a good press). They may not be much fun to be around, but they have stability and contact. (2) Escalate: A: "If you don't go to the movies, I'll punch your face." B: "Punch me, and I'll murder you in your sleep." Paul Watzlawick has coined the wonderful term "escalating schismogenic symmetry" for this condition. It is analogous to an arms race in which the parties pour most of their resources into making escalating threats credible. The loss of these resources makes each feel even more vulnerable—which requires stronger defenses. This way lies depletion or disaster—probably both. Not an attractive option. (3) Terminate the relationship. Stable symmetry is frustrating, and escalating symmetry is frustrating and dangerous, so A and B, finding no satisfaction in each other's company, can split and find others to argue with:

Movies	Dancing	Movies	Dancing
(A)——→	←——(D)	(B)——→	←——(C)

(4) Move to Complementarity.

The complementary relationship is the second form of power relationship. It can be formed when either A or B agrees to let the other set the context.

> Let's go to the
> Movies   (A)↘
>   ↖(B) O.K.

This seems to be a promising move, but its result is still uncertain. The outcome becomes more clear on the next date. If A agrees that the couple should dance this time because they went to the movies last time, the relationship becomes mutually complementary:

Ⓐ Movies Ⓑ Dancing
＼↑ ＼↑
Ⓑ O.K. Ⓐ O.K.

This is a picture of a healthy relationship. Each feels the ability to set the context when each needs to and the safety to let the other set it as well. There will usually be some unstated rules governing who sets the context for when, and how transitions are made. Anyone you are happy to see approaching you is a person with whom you have a mutually complementary relationship.

Sometimes in some of these relationships, intimacy is achieved. Intimacy is the third power relationship and can be defined as a relationship in which, for the moment, power is irrelevant. Ⓐ I'm Here, Ⓑ I'm Here. This can happen when two people feel safe and sufficiently in contact that there is no need to control the context. Sexual intercourse is sometimes euphemistically called "intimate relations." This is somewhat appropriate, because when things are going well, a feedback system emerges so that A's pleasure gives B pleasure and vice versa. At such a time, neither feels the need to control the other and in fact is strongly impelled to please the other. And then it's over, and it was wonderful, and then A wants to read, and B can't sleep with the light on, and the struggle for the context resumes. This example is not merely cynicism, but an effort to point out that intimacy is not stable; rather, it is a part of some mutually complementary relationship. The parting after intimacy keeps the intimacy possible, for too much closeness threatens differentiation and autonomy and is as intolerable as too much isolation.

Mutual complementarity and intimacy are not, however, the problem—although they may be the solution. If we return to our couple A and B as they meet for their next date after B agreed to go to the movies the week before, A, confident from the past week's success, is all set to go to the movies again. After all, remember how much fun they had last time! A is now trying to impose unilateral complementarity. B is now faced with the following options: (1) Move back to symmetry. This gets back to fighting. If A can be made to see the wisdom of mutual complementarity—wonderful. Somehow it is doubtful that A will catch on. In which case B can fight to exhaustion or disaster, or (2) terminate. Probably a wise option if possible, or (3) give in again. Imagine if during the fight A presented B with a credible ultimatum threatening violence if B did not agree to go to the movies. Assuming that in B's eyes this escalation makes continued symmetry too dangerous and terminating is not an option, it would appear that capitulation is B's only option. The advantage to B's accepting a unilaterally complementary relationship with A is obvious: stability and physical safety. There are always secure positions open for anyone who is willing to do whatever another person wants.

The disadvantages, however, are significant. Over time, regardless of how well B can rationalize the situation, B will begin to feel secondary. "There are hammers and anvils; I am but an anvil. My reward will be in heaven." B's energy level and intelligence will decline. B will lose self-esteem, which loss will make further surrender less painful, until B stands in danger of losing a sense of self entirely. The choice between a dangerous escalating symmetry and a unilateral complementarity is far from an attractive one. Happily, such is the human spirit that when faced with such a dilemma, it will—consciously or not—invent a third alternative. This alternative is the fourth and, from a clinical point of view, most interesting power state, Pseudocomplementarity. This obviously means that it looks complementary, but it's not. It can be diagrammed thus:

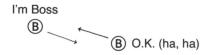

Notice that B is in no way claiming the right to set the context. A's power is unchallenged—but there is a catch. B, for example, agrees to go to the movies, but on the way develops a cough which continues through the entire film. B tries to stop coughing, eagerly trying every solution suggested by A but with no success. Finally B might say, "I'm spoiling this for you" and stand in the back of the theater, still coughing loudly. The next week it happens again. A has the right to set the context and force B to go to the movies any time. B willingly accepts A's power without challenge or rebellion, indeed makes every effort to follow A's wishes—but somehow this situation holds little satisfaction for A.

It is unlikely that there are many living people who have not experienced pseudocomplementarity from both positions, and the B experience is universal. Members of groups often designated as powerless or secondary—blacks, women, Spanish-speaking people, and all children and adolescents—become highly skilled at pseudocomplementarity, although even white, educated, Anglo-Saxon males are usually afforded many opportunities to practice it.

A U.S. senator or even a president faced with an embarrassing question from a reporter generally will not say, "I won't answer that," or "That question is stupid and insulting." After all, symmetry is dangerous for the bigger person, too, for if you win, you are a bully and if you lose, you are a bum. Also, reporters have the "right" to question public officials. The common strategy for the senator is to "misunderstand" the question and answer the question as misunderstood. At less lofty levels, blacks sometimes find it convenient to be "stupid, lazy, and shiftless," women to be "impractical, incompetent, and hysterical," Hispanics to be "uncomprehending, alien, and obtuse," and children "deaf, naive, and ignorant." Just as judo uses the momentum of an opponent to render him or her helpless, pseudocongruence can use the insulting assumptions of others to cancel whatever power the other may have. In the absence of a person attempting to dominate them, however, most blacks recover their intelligence, women their competence, Hispanics their savvy, and children their sentience.

For them pseudocongruence is a strategy applied with at least some consciousness in the context where they are, in the view of the strategist, appropriate.

There is another type of pseudocongruence, however, that is not under conscious control. The name given to this type of behavior is a "symptom." This name is, in one sense, unfortunate, because it drags up a whole host of implications from the medical model. In another sense the choice is apt, because it brings into sharp focus the differences between the assumptions of traditional psychodynamically oriented therapy and strategic systems-oriented therapy.

To a medically trained person the word *symptom* means "the external sign of a disease." There is some implication that the cure may be applied with little direct relationship to the symptom, since the symptom is merely serving to indicate that disease is present and is not central to the disease. Treating the symptom was, and still is, a scornful term applied by traditional psychiatry to unsophisticated treatment. It was seen as analogous to treating measles by applying makeup to the spots.

The systems-oriented therapist defines a symptom as any behavior which has the following two characteristics: It controls or defines the context in which interaction takes place, and it directly or indirectly makes the claim "I can't help it." Rather than being the condition of an individual, the symptom is an interactional event.

A tree falling in the woods out of the earshot of a witness may or may not make a sound. From a systems point of view there is an implied answer to that ancient controversy: a symptom does not exist until it acts on another person. A person may think he is Jesus Christ in private and remain symptom free; only when he makes this claim to another does he have a symptom.

To illustrate how a symptom works, let us imagine A and B about to meet on a blind date. B has given a detailed personal description on the phone and so does not have the option of claiming not to be B. As A introduces himself, B notices that A has a pronounced stutter.

Consider B's dilemma. The available options seem to be: (1) going on the date; (2) refusing to go, accepting the role of the "bad guy" and the guilt which accompanies it; (3) producing a countersymptom, like claiming to have a headache.

If B adopts the third option and claims a headache, A may accept this gracefully and withdraw or say something like, "All my dates get headaches when they see me. I guess you are disappointed with me. You don't have to go out with me if you don't want to."

B's position seems to boil down to a choice of leaving and feeling guilty or staying and feeling oppressed. Moreover, as everyone who has had an unsuccessful blind date knows, it is very hard to say, "Look, I don't think that this is going to work out. Why don't we just quit now and cut our losses?" It is not easy to reject someone and take responsibility for hurting him or her. In this case A could accept B's headache story and withdraw or push without making any statement about B. B had to commit with no commitment from A. Who is in charge here?

Anyone who has ever interacted with someone who was delusional or depressed knows the feeling of helplessness that accompanies such encounters. Even though it is the other person who is "sick," most people feel overwhelmed. The normally accepted rules of human intercourse do not apply in such situations, and there is no clear substitute set of rules. The new rules must come from the person who suspended the old ones, and that person thereby sets the context. The other person often feels both responsible for the welfare of the person with the symptom and totally helpless to take care of himself or herself.

All the symptom can really do is paralyze the power of others and sometimes force them into a resentful caretaking role. In addition, there is little satisfaction for the person with the symptom. The price of a symptom is that the victim may be considered—by both self and others—as sick, marginal, and perhaps even an object of scorn and pity. This makes the power derived expensive indeed.

Now a logical implication of the proposed definition of a

symptom is that the two characteristics are both necessary and sufficient for a behavior to function as a symptom, which means that if a behavior either (a) failed to control the context of interaction or (b) was admitted to be voluntary, then it would not operate as a symptom. This would change the economics of the behavior from being one which produces power without responsibility but is very expensive, to being one which produces nothing but remains just as expensive. In such an economic climate, the behavior is unlikely to survive.

The question, of course, is how can one affect a symptom so that its interpersonal effect is altered?

The therapeutic strategies and tactics of systems therapy are aimed at changing the transactional context in which behavior occurs. In planning an intervention a therapist, rather than trying to figure out why a behavior occurs, merely observes what happens when a behavior occurs and contrives to change that. Not only does this simplify and radically enhance the effectiveness of treatment, but it also simplifies and makes much more useful the process of diagnosis.

For example, the one "illness" that causes more hospital stays than any other condition in this country is called schizophrenia. If one were to ask twenty clinicians of any training for a definition of this word, one would be sure to get twenty different definitions. With this kind of confusion as to what it is, one can imagine the confusion as to what causes it. Convincing arguments have been made for genetic, biochemical, microorganism, spiritual, and interactional causes. My own guess is that all of these factors are probably involved. It is important to point out that the diagnosis "schizophrenic" in no way facilitates treatment, because it does not define the condition in such a way that a clear treatment strategy is initiated. A group of investigators led by the anthropologist-philosopher Gregory Bateson and including John Weakland, Don D. Jackson, and Jay Haley examined instead what the symptoms labeled schizophrenic do in systems where they are exhibited, and they found that all the labeled varieties of symptoms—hebephrenic, paranoid, dissociated, catatonic, or affective—do the same thing: they prevent contact by claiming, "I am not communicating." If I claim to be Jesus Christ, you have the option of communicating with Jesus, but not with me. The group, therefore, investigated interpersonal tactics that would stop the symptoms from preventing contact and relieving the symptomholder of responsibility for communication.

A good example of these kinds of tactics is a story Jay Haley tells of Milton Erickson in *Uncommon Therapy*. When Erickson was a teaching fellow at Worcester State Hospital he introduced himself to a patient who responded, "I am Jesus Christ."

Erickson asked, "Is it true you are dedicated to helping others?"

"It is," the patient replied.

"I understand you have a background in carpentry," said Erickson. "I need a bookcase very badly. Could you make me one?"

Just as the judo player utilizes the strength of an opponent, Erickson utilized the symptom of the patient to make good contact with him and to get the patient involved in constructive work. In the context set by Erickson, the patient's delusion did not function as a symptom, and indeed soon vanished, costing the world one savior and the hospital one patient. Another more detailed example of a therapist using a delusional symptom to facilitate contact and end the delusions can be found in Joanne Greenberg's *I Never Promised You a Rose Garden* (first published under the name of Hannah Green).

Seeing this in terms of communication theory, Erickson placed the patient in a double bind—a move to define the context as one where the patient is forced to choose between unacceptable alternatives. If he is Jesus Christ, he is also a helper and a carpenter and must deal with Erickson. If he is not Jesus Christ, then he is someone else to whom Erickson must relate. The option of not relating is not present.

A less elegant example comes from my own practice. A patient had a bad stutter and requested help with it. I asked him to stutter on every word. When he missed words, I asked him to repeat the sentence, remembering to stutter on each word. This change of context stopped the stutter from functioning as a symptom because: (1) It no longer controlled the context. I was ordering him to stutter. (2) He could not claim ''I can't help it.'' He was stuttering on purpose at my request. Within three weeks his stutter was barely detectable.

When a therapist prescribes or predicts a symptom, it changes the pseudocongruent character of the behavior and forces congruence:

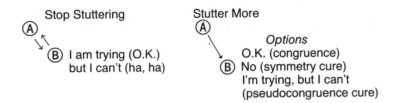

The only way B can avoid congruence is to stop stuttering. The symptom no longer pays off in preventing domination and threat to self. Such a move is called a ''paradoxical injunction'' for it places the receiver in a paradoxical situation of having to drop the trusted antidomination strategy to avoid domination.

The Gregory Bateson group hypothesized familial double binding as a contributor to ''schizophrenic'' symptoms. A thorough discussion of this phenomenon is not relevant to this work. But in passing, consider the options of a child who is told by a parent, ''You listen to others too much. I want you to stop following other people's instructions and become more independent, and I want you to start right now.'' One possible solution is to not be the person addressed.

Although these ideas were developed while studying the symptoms associated with schizophrenia, they also apply to the symptoms which develop in a system consistently exposed to drunkenness. The power struggles in an alcoholic family are more blatant and gross than in what Mara Selvini Palazzoli calls ''families in schizophrenic transaction,'' but similar approaches to treatment apply.

The most common complaints clinicians make about alcoholic families is that they are so resistant to change. A therapist seeing an alcoholic's wife, for example, might repeatedly urge her not to give her husband drinking money, only to hear that (a) he steals it from her purse; (b) he will get violent if she withholds it; (c) he might steal if she withholds it; or (d) it's his money, he earns it, and she just can't keep it from him. The therapist is in the position of arguing with the client who is supposedly an ally.

(A) Withhold money.

   (B) I should (O.K.),
       but I can't (ha, ha)

The implied metacommunication in this interaction might go:

(A) You know what you should do, but you won't do it. You're a bad patient.

   (B) I'm stupid and cowardly. I'll never learn.

With the feelings:

(A) You frustrate my need to be competent and successful!

   (B) I'm trying so hard. You don't understand me and make me feel stupid and bad and to blame for my husband's drinking. You are just like him!

If the goal is to empower the wife so that she feels strong enough to risk making changes, the above process seems doomed to failure.

If this is not enough, the therapist is facing an additional trap in denying the wife's reality. Apart from invalidating her perception, making her feel weak and stupid, and indeed giving messages identical to those her husband gives her, the therapist is also committing himself to what may be a dangerous distortion of reality. What if, for example, he finally got the wife to withhold money and the husband broke her nose. Such an incident might adversely affect the future therapeutic relationship, to say the least.

This is a common trap. Observers of communication have often noted that the process is more important than the content. If the process is the therapist suggesting changes and the wife giving reasons why they are impossible,* the process of struggle will supersede the merit of the wife's reasons. What is important is that the therapist is right and the wife wrong. About *what* is secondary. The wife's resistance to the therapist dominating her also transcends the context.

The wife's resistance to the therapist is not unhealthy. It is hard to feel enthusiastic about her trading domination by her husband for domination by a therapist. Unfortunately her passive, pseudocongruent style of resistance teaches her nothing new. If the therapist were to change tactics, however, we might see a different picture:

w: It makes me so mad at myself that I give him money to drink with.

T: What would happen if you didn't?

w: I'm afraid he might hit me.

T: That sounds like too big a chance to take. You'd better keep giving him the money.

w: But he hits me anyway.

T: Maybe you're not giving him enough money.

w: I'm not sure that's it. That doesn't make any sense.

T: No?

As the therapist allies with the resistance—in this case very legitimate concerns—more of the independence and creativity of the client are mobilized. Indeed, she finds herself arguing enthusiastically against her own rationalization for continued powerlessness and inaction.

Apart from efficacy, this approach is preferable even if it doesn't lead to immediate action. In the first situation described, the client is caught in an antitherapeutic double-bind. If she

---

*Eric Berne calls this the "Why Don't You—Yes But" game. *Games People Play*, p. 116.

resists change, she remains in an intolerable position, whereas if she changes, she does so at the behest of the therapist and therefore cannot feel independent in her moves for independence, but rather feels more beholden to the therapist to tell her what to do. In the second instance, if she doesn't change, at least she can feel supported and in an alliance with her therapist rather than guilty and unsuccessful. The therapist remains a resource and has not defined himself as ineffective and unsupportive by unsuccessfully selling her changes she is not ready to make.

If, on the other hand, she hears her arguments and acts upon them, she totally owns the changes she has made and earns a measure of independence from the therapist, who cautioned her against them. Her healthy resistance to authority in this case works therapeutically.

In these examples I made the therapist a male to point up the similarities between his dysfunctional role and that of the client's husband, and also to show how a transference would work in the client's favor in the second instance. A woman therapist, however, can fall into authority traps quite as easily. Rather than becoming an invalidating male, a female therapist can be set up as an unattainable role model and be equally disempowering.

Many people object to the paradoxical approach on ethical grounds, claiming that such a stance is tricky, cynical, dishonest, and contemptuous of clients. In my opinion, nothing could be farther from the truth. More ''direct'' therapeutic approaches work on the premise that the client is incompetent and the therapist, with superior knowledge and training, must guide the client in making wise decisions. The therapist will debunk or confront the client's ''sick,'' ''primitive,'' or ''mistaken'' ideas and introduce more ''rational'' and ''mature'' concepts. Apart from being contemptuous of the client, such an approach infantilizes the client and maintains dependency on the therapist.

The paradoxical stance also allows the therapist always to

tell the truth—not the whole truth, perhaps—but at no time must the therapist say anything he or she does not fully believe to be true. One exercise often assigned to therapists training to do strategic family therapy is to have them frame the headlines from the first three pages of a newspaper in sincerely positive terms. Reframing these headlines—"Thousands Starving in Cambodia," "Reagan and Carter Win Again"—provides a challenge for the beginning student. Once the students really understand that absolutely everything cuts both ways and that the storms that washed out your picnic also saved some farmer's crop, they can handle any of these headlines with aplomb. The starvation in Cambodia headline, for example can be reframed as such:

"The sickening situation in Cambodia may finally demonstrate to the superpowers, particularly the U.S., the outcome of promiscuous intervention into alien cultures. Cambodia is going to make it much harder to justify similar adventures on the rationale of saving "the people" from anything. It is hard to imagine any situation which is not preferable to the results of our intervention in Southeast Asia. In addition, the plight of the Cambodians is so dramatic and heart rending that relief efforts cross ideological boundaries and provide factions usually in conflict with an opportunity to cooperate and build trust, thereby making peace more likely in the future."

Now I believe the above statement sincerely. I recognize that the proportions are distorted, and that the benefits listed are bought at a bizarre price. In the context of an alcoholic family the benefits a therapist might cite are also bought at a bizarre price, but one must remember that one is talking to people who have been routinely paying that price for years. Hearing the therapist do this gives the family a chance to consciously consider the trade-offs they have been choosing automatically up to now. Telling a mother that it is very frightening to risk angering the father in order to protect a child gives the mother a chance to consciously evaluate the conflict, while it also validates and dignifies the fears and problems on which she has based her previous decision. The therapist should not have the power to decide what risks others should take. What often seems like an intolerably pathological situation to a therapist is the everyday reality of the client. No one will listen to someone who does not validate his or her reality. Bandler and Grinder in *Structure of Magic* stress the importance of "pacing and leading" a client, emphasizing that you must join the client where he or she is before you can hope to lead the client to someplace new.

When, therefore, a mother is faced with a therapist who provides rationales for the status quo and reasons why change is difficult, if not impossible, she is forced to consciously realize the gravity of the problem. This motivates her to look critically at the therapist's rationalizations and conservatism.

It is to be hoped that her behavior will begin to change spontaneously, making life much less smooth for the alcoholic. It is one experience to get drunk and pass out in the living room and then awake in one's bed in clean pajamas. It is quite another if one wakes at four A.M. in a pile on the living room floor, lying in the mess of the night before. If this begins happening, the alcoholic becomes motivated to examine his drinking or at least join the counseling process in order to sabotage it. This same process applies if the wife comes in alone, although if the paradox is applied to a child as well as the wife, then two members of the family become conscious, enhancing the chance of success.

When working with any system, concepts like "sick," "psychotic," and "pathological" can entrap therapists into dysfunction. If a behavior is sick it is by definition irrational, destructive, unhealthy, and bad. Clearly no one in his or her right mind would perform such a behavior intentionally, and therefore, such behaviors are identified as beyond the client's control, perpetrated by some part of the client possessed by evil or pathology and inaccessible to rational process.

Another important aspect of such terms is that they are disapproving, critical, and uncomplimentary. Regardless of motivation, criticism is seldom constructive. If you have a habit which you define as bad: smoking, overeating, or nail-biting, for example, it is seldom helpful to have the unpleasant aspects of them pointed out, even by people who "mean well."

"Gosh! Do you really need another cigarette? They're so bad for you!" is not the kind of statement likely to help someone stop smoking. However well-meaning the statement, it (a) sets the speaker up as more knowledgeable and rational than the smoker, (b) implies that the smoker is either ignorant or unconcerned about his (her) health, (c) implies that the smoker doesn't need cigarettes but is merely weak and self-indulgent, and (d) puts the speaker in a parental role with the responsibility of passing judgment on the smoker's behavior. By stopping smoking, the smoker is, in effect, endorsing these implications.

Such statements are often defended with the argument that they make the smoker conscious of his (her) behavior. The premise that "bad" habits do not usually involve conscious decisions is a sound one. Smokers seldom make a conscious decision to light up. The problem with this argument is that the smoker will become more conscious of the criticism than the behavior and will often light up as a gesture of defiance or out of the anxiety generated by the criticism. Smoking, therefore, becomes a friend who protects one from domination.

Confrontation of negative behavior—be it social, hygienic, or political—has a very good press. People are encouraged in advice columns and support groups to confront boors, bullies, chauvinists, and oppressors. This advice tends to be given by people not affected by the outcome, which is seldom positive. Most frequently the confronted behavior does not change, and if it does, it changes at unacceptable expense.

My experience has shown confrontation to be an effective tactic in only two situations. (1) In the context of intimacy, where the person confronted has assurance that the confrontation is motivated by concern and respect, and (2) when the confronter has the power to dictate the context and to enforce compliance. Obviously the latter situation is vulnerable to pseudocongruent strategies. Just as important, oppressors must always sleep with one eye open, as must rescuers, for if the power balance changes for any reason, other tactics are going to have to be found fast.

The alternative to confrontation and the symmetry which often results is the "positive frame." The assumption behind this technique is that behavior has no absolute value and can be positive or negative depending on the contextual frame. Therefore, if a behavior is present in a system, that system must possess some context in which the behavior is useful and positive. The therapist will then frame everything that occurs in a positive light.

If a son gets arrested for drunk driving, for example, the therapist might frame this as an attempt to ally the parents through a clear expression that he needs more effective limits. The fact that the parents respond to the arrest by blaming each other might be defined as the parents' holding onto their individual theories of child rearing in spite of the son's attempt to produce crisis.

What happens then is that the goal of confrontation is achieved—the family must become conscious of its behavior and make a considered choice about it, while the major drawback of confrontation is avoided. The family does not have the opportunity to respond defensively to being criticized and thereby avoid the content. Not only must the family become aware of its behavior and make a choice about it, but that choice must necessarily be influenced by the power relationship with the therapist. For instance, in the above example, the family can accept the frame that the boy is trying to get more limits or not. If so, then it is clear that the family needs a strategy and skills for providing limits or must accept the fact that the parents don't want to provide limits. If the family argues with the frame, what can they offer as an alternative? Perhaps that the boy is inherently a bad actor who, in spite of their skillful and dedicated parenting, persists in misbehaving. Or maybe the boy is fine, but drugs and ill-chosen companions are responsible for his current naughtiness? Perchance the boy has outgrown his ability to take parenting? With all of these the therapist will agree, merely holding the family responsible for the logical implications. If the child is an evil changeling, then he must be banished, but he can no longer provide the parents with a convenient distraction from their own problems and conflict. If the child is an innocent victim of drug pur- veyors and other riffraff, that only points up the need for more effective limits and protection. If the child cannot be con- trolled, then he is to be applauded for his cleverness in work- ing out a living arrangement in which he is getting material support without onerous limits or responsibilities, whereas the parents are exemplary for their unquestioning generosity and self-sacrifice.

This strategy allows everyone in the family to perceive events and sequences in a new way, without arousing their usual information-rejecting defenses. When the therapist places in a positive frame sequences of behavior which are part of a dys- functional strategy, then the family continuing these behaviors will not set up a feeling of failure in the family or (very impor- tant) in the therapist. If the family cannot fail, then the thera- pist is not inclined to berate the family for not taking sage advice. This makes it harder for the therapist to fall into per- secuting the family, which is the inevitable game position Res- cuers move to in the Rescue Triangle.

If, however, the family must resist the power of the thera- pist, the only way it can do so is to abandon the dysfunctional sequence and do something else. This is not so bad either. It is much harder for the family to persist in the dysfunctional sequence once it is consciously aware of it. In spite of the therapist's enthusiasm, each member of the family will notice several negative aspects of the sequence, often quite sponta- neously.

It is safe to generalize that human communication is full of ambivalence. If someone supports one side of a question, one's first reaction may be to think of the other. For example, if you say to someone, "You're sure lucky to be married," you are likely to hear about some negative aspect of married life. This is a natural defense against accepting someone else's definition of reality without checking it out. In tightly bonded groups, like enmeshed, overinvolved families, this effect is multiplied.

This counterdefinition reaction, however, is not universal. Some families—particularly confused, disorganized, disengaged families—are looking for someone to define the situation and are eager to accept that definition. If a therapist sees this to be the case, it is safe to make direct suggestions. Salvador Minuchin explores this subject extensively in *Families of the Slums,* in which he presents strategies for working with disengaged, multiproblem families.

Earlier I stated that there are three major contexts in which the alcoholic family comes into treatment: through the children, through the wife, and through the alcoholic. Within these contexts there are three major stages around which a treatment plan is developed. These are: (a) while the drinking is still active, (b) early sobriety, and (c) when drinking is no longer an issue. Because in the latter case the family no longer requires special techniques, only (a) and (b) will be discussed here.

The strategy in (a) involves gaining contact with as much of the family as possible. Realistically this usually means the child who attracted attention and the mother. In rare cases the mother's assistant is available as well. The father almost never appears for early sessions.

Whether the referral is from the court, the school, or a mental health worker, it is safe to assume that, although there is genuine concern for the child, the family will be reluctant to stay in treatment any longer than is necessary to placate the referring agency. One can assume further that no one in the family is likely to be forthcoming about the real nature of the problem (if they are consciously aware of it at all). A therapist may have a suspicion about the nature of the family from an evaluation of the child, but especially if the mother fits the profile as well, it is useful to operate from the working hypothesis that the family is alcoholic. It may turn out that the father is not alcoholic, but if both the mother and child fit the described profiles, then the father is seriously disengaged and inoperative, and tactics designed for alcoholic families will be appropriate.

In the first family (mother and child) interview, the therapist's focus will be on the mother. Treating the child without making fundamental changes in the family system will be a losing battle, as the child (other than a mother's assistant) is not sufficiently pivotal to the family structure to provide the therapist with enough leverage to cause change. The mother, however, is absolutely necessary to the continued smooth functioning of the family. Therefore, if the therapist can significantly impede the mother from playing her role in the system, it will upset the precarious balance of the whole system.

It is important to note here that before positive changes can be made in these families, it is necessary to first sabotage their normal functioning; therefore, early moves will be directed at upsetting the usual sequences of interaction, causing confusion and discomfort. This is going to be painful to both the family and the therapist, and the temptation to avoid this pain will be great. The therapist can be bolstered against this temptation by visualizing what will befall the family members if the current patterns continue unchanged.

The mother in such a family is caught between her strong moral feelings of responsibility for the welfare of her children and fear of change. Her desire to protect her children is paralyzed by her need to protect her husband and his right to drink. Her fear of her husband and any change in his role is in conflict with her anger and moral judgments. It is these conflicts which the therapist must exploit to sabotage the system.

It is useful to think of a client's behavior as representing a point on a continuum of conflicting impulses:

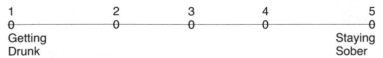

The conflict between drunk and sober, for example, could be represented as a line drawn between the two extreme positions. Point (1) represents a person who is either drinking or unconscious from drinking at any given moment, and point (5) represents a recovered alcoholic or someone else who will not drink under any circumstances. A person at point (2) is drinking destructively. My assumption is that it will be more effective to ask this person why he is not a point (1) drinker than to delineate the advantages of points (3), (4), or (5).

An alcoholic's wife who is attending a conference about her disturbed child has many conflicts simultaneously:

	Where she is at present
Concern for Child	Fear of Change— Feels Helpless
────────────────── X ──────────────────	
Anger and Contempt for Husband	Fear of and Dependence on Husband
────────────────── X ──────────────────	
Hatred of Drinking	Fear of Change
────────────────── X ──────────────────	

A therapist hoping to move her attitudes in a positive direction would be well advised to become the voice of her fear and helplessness. If she becomes exasperated with her husband and says something like "I'm fed up with his drinking and lying; I won't put up with it anymore," the inexperienced therapist might encourage those sentiments; the more experienced therapist, however, might counter with: "At least you know what you're dealing with. Besides, are things really that bad now?"

If, as previously proposed, the therapist is able to infect the wife with some consciousness about her situation, her behavior will change, and this will spread the infection to the home. One prophylactic measure often taken by the husband at this time is to join the therapeutic process. This event is usually heralded by ominous rumblings such as "My husband wants me to stop coming here," or "My husband is pretty mad at me for listening to you. He says you're making trouble between us." If the therapist misperceives the wife as an ally and the husband as the "problem," then this move might lock the therapist into a highly dysfunctional alliance with the wife against the husband.

This trap can be avoided by allying with the wife's fear and resistance. It is irresponsible indeed to force the wife to choose between her husband and her therapist. If the husband has threatened to hurt the wife if she continues therapy, this irresponsibility can reach the level of malpractice. Therefore it is not only strategically effective, but ethically necessary for the therapist to say, "If this process is dangerous to you or your marriage, maybe it should be discontinued." If the wife leaves therapy at that point (which has happened only once in my experience), then she leaves with the memory of a therapist who took her needs and fears seriously. If, on the other hand, she decides to accept the risk and stay, she accepts full responsibility and cannot play the therapist and her husband off against each other. The therapist also can inquire why the husband is so upset in light of the fact that the therapist has never urged the wife to do anything to which he would object. A possible explanation which the therapist might offer is that the husband misunderstands what is going on in therapy. This explanation might lead to the suggestion that the wife explain the process to her husband in some detail. At this point the wife often claims either that her husband is not interested (which makes his objections hard to fathom) or she can't make him understand.

The therapist has a clear goal at this point: to bring the husband into treatment. It can be assumed that the system will throw up many ingenious barriers. No matter how angry or concerned the wife is and how much she would like her husband to get help—or at least be publicly exposed for his irresponsible behavior—she is also justly fearful of a confrontation with him in front of a therapist. These fears have varied content. Some of the more common are: (1) The therapist will come to believe her husband's claim that he drinks because she is such a bitch; (2) the therapist will no longer think she is important once confronted with her husband's more serious problems; (3) the therapist will say that she has exaggerated her husband's problem; (4a) a female therapist will be charmed by her seductive husband; (4b) a male therapist will ally with her husband; (5) the therapist will fail, dashing her hopes; and (6) her husband will humiliate her by revealing information which she is not ready to make known. This list is by no means exhaustive but may provide some insight into why the wife might not be as potent an ally for bringing the husband in as the therapist might have hoped. There is some temptation for the therapist to make light of these fears out of frustration. This communicates to the wife that she is not understood or that her feelings are invalid and leaves her alone in the task of protecting herself from her fears.

Therefore, once the therapist begins to suspect the rationale for the wife's resistance, the wise course is to emphasize or even exaggerate the potential problems. Also, if the therapist feels an anxiety about meeting the husband, who might be irate and will certainly be a challenge to both skill and self-esteem—then the therapist ought to reexamine the situation. Anxiety accompanies every change, no matter how welcome or appropriate. It is often useful for the therapist to share this anxiety and allow the wife, an expert on helping, to help. With the therapist stressing the problems associated with bringing the husband into the treatment process, the wife is free either to delay bringing him without fighting the therapist or to solve the problems with the therapist's support.

Putting this into practice might produce an interview like the following:

WIFE: I'm very worried.

THERAPIST: Worried?

WIFE: I think my husband is an alcoholic.

THERAPIST: What makes you think that?

WIFE: He goes out after dinner and gets drunk almost every night.

THERAPIST: What do you mean drunk?

WIFE: He comes home and bumps into things and talks all

slurred. Once, last week, he drove the car up on the lawn.

THERAPIST: You two haven't been getting along too well recently, have you?

WIFE: I'll say.

THERAPIST: Well, maybe it's just as well he goes out nights. He leaves you to yourself. (Positive frame.) Besides, his drinking doesn't hurt you.

WIFE: Well, I'm afraid it's hurting him.

THERAPIST: What do you care? I thought you were mad at him.

WIFE: Well, I love him, too.

THERAPIST: So what do you think you ought to do? Have you mentioned it to him?

WIFE: No, I'm afraid to.

THERAPIST: Yeah, he'd probably get real mad and defensive. It may not be worth it.

WIFE: Maybe I shouldn't let him take the car.

THERAPIST: How could you stop him?

WIFE: I could hide the keys.

THERAPIST: You're afraid to say anything for fear he'll get mad, and now you're going to hide the car keys? My guess is he'll really get mad then!

WIFE: Well, what should I do? Do you think he's an alcoholic?

THERAPIST: I won't say. I don't have enough information. You've got to admit you're not an unbiased observer.

WIFE: You mean you've got to talk to him? He'll never come in.

THERAPIST: You're probably right.

WIFE: Besides, if I even mentioned it to him, he'd kill me.

THERAPIST: It sounds like it's too scary to even bring it up now.

WIFE: But I worry.

THERAPIST: Well, there are lots of things that we worry about but can't do anything about. I worry there's going to be an atomic war.

WIFE: It's not the same thing! Harry is my husband. He should come in and talk to you!

THERAPIST: What good would that do?

WIFE: You're an expert. You could talk to him. You could make him see that he's killing himself.

THERAPIST: I'm flattered you have such faith in me, but it sounds like a tall order. Besides, are you sure you really want him to come in? I'm your therapist, you know, not his. This has been your private space. Are you sure you would want to share it with him? (This is shameless manipulation. Therapist knows that Wife has strong moral convictions against selfishness and putting her needs first.)

WIFE: He needs to talk to someone, and I have faith in you.

THERAPIST: I appreciate your confidence, but as you say, he'll never come in.

WIFE: We'll see.

If the wife becomes less ambivalent about including the husband in treatment, he will almost certainly have to deal with the therapist. The first encounter often takes place on the phone. Because the therapist, rather than engaging the wife to bring him in, has been stressing the problems and doubts regarding the husband coming into treatment, there is considerable flexibility available when he calls.

HUSBAND: Hello. Is this Dr. T?

THERAPIST: Yes, can I help you?

HUSBAND: I don't know. You've been seeing my wife, Mrs. H, for a couple of months.

THERAPIST: She told you that?

HUSBAND: Yeah, and I'm not sure the sessions have been helpful.

THERAPIST: No?

HUSBAND: No. She's acting weird and getting on my case, and I don't like it.

THERAPIST: Getting on your case?

HUSBAND: Yeah, she's doing all kinds of weird stuff. She says I'm an alcoholic.

THERAPIST: She does?

HUSBAND: Yeah, do you think I'm an alcoholic?

THERAPIST: Me? Why ask me?

HUSBAND: She seems to think you know what you're talking about, and I bet she talks about me a lot.

THERAPIST: Well, I obviously can't make judgments on the basis of one-sided imformation.

HUSBAND: What do you mean? What does she say about me?

THERAPIST: You must realize I can't talk about that.

HUSBAND: Why? She's my wife. I ought to come in to get things straight.

THERAPIST: I'm not sure whether that would be appropriate. I'd need her permission.

One can imagine how unsatisfying it must be to talk to Dr. T. He sounds just like a shrink. This kind of approach raises curiosity without raising anxiety. Questions like "Why would she think you are an alcoholic?" are best saved for the consultation room. Being withholding without being challenging will convey the message that while the therapist is not particularly eager to see the husband, it is negotiable, and the husband will feel that he can handle the therapist if he does come in.

The conjoint interview of an alcoholic couple is a tricky business. The therapist is faced with many seemingly contradictory tasks which must be simultaneously attended to. On the one hand the primary client is most likely the wife, who must not be betrayed but not allied with either. On the other hand the alcoholic must not be confronted, yet must be forced to deal with his drinking—and all of this must be done in a way that leaves them both motivated to return. This can be accomplished by applying the principles already described (positive framing and paradox). The following interview is an abbreviated version of an actual interview:

WIFE: Dr. T., this is my husband, Harry.

THERAPIST: Pleased to meet you.

HUSBAND: Hi.

THERAPIST: What can I do for you?

HUSBAND: You can get her off my back.

WIFE: (loudly) Off your back! With your boss calling me telling me you're drunk on the job? What are we going to do if you get fired? Off your back!

HUSBAND: I don't drink on the job, and I don't get drunk.

THERAPIST: Your wife seems to think she can control your drinking.

HUSBAND: Well, she can't. Besides I don't drink much anyway.

THERAPIST: Even if you did, there's no way she can control it. It's not her business.

WIFE: Not my business! What are the kids and I going to do if he loses his job?

THERAPIST: Well, if it's your business, get him to drink less.

WIFE: I can't.

THERAPIST: Exactly! (to Husband) She can't control your drinking. You can drink as much as you want.

WIFE: Well, if he drinks as much as he wants, he'll lose his job. His boss says he's getting fed up.

HUSBAND: He couldn't have said that. I never get drunk at work.

THERAPIST: You mean he's lying?

HUSBAND: No, she just misunderstood him.

THERAPIST: (to Wife) Your husband seems adamant on this point. Is it possible you misunderstood?

WIFE: No, he said that Harry was drunk on the job twice this week and that he always smells of booze, and if it keeps up, he will have to let him go.

THERAPIST: (to Husband) Wow! That seems pretty cut and dried.

HUSBAND: Well, it's not so!

THERAPIST: You mean your boss is telling your wife lies about you behind your back? That's defamation of character and alienation of affections. You could sue him for plenty.

HUSBAND: Uh, I'm sure it's a misunderstanding.

THERAPIST: I hope you're right. I'm surprised you don't find this more upsetting than you seem to. You must be extraordinarily charitable.

HUSBAND: Yeah. Live and let live. [Ironically this is an A.A. slogan.]

THERAPIST: It seems your boss doesn't share your philosophy. Even so, I bet you're tempted to just let this go and not do anything about it.

HUSBAND: Well . . . Yeah. That seems best.

THERAPIST: The only problem is that doing nothing implies that the accusations are true. God knows what he will say next. I can understand your reluctance to defend yourself. He is your boss and all, but if I were you, I'd be too scared to let it go. Especially if you're right about this.

HUSBAND: Right about what?

THERAPIST: About this being a misunderstanding.

HUSBAND: Oh!

THERAPIST: Think you'll talk to your boss before we meet again?

HUSBAND: Uh, yeah.

THERAPIST: I can't see you until next Wednesday. Is that okay?

HUSBAND: Uh, yeah.

THERAPIST: (to Wife) Will you want to come, too?

WIFE: Oh, sure, I'll be here!

THERAPIST: (to Husband) She thinks you're not going to show.

HUSBAND: Oh, I'll be here.

THERAPIST: But I bet you're tempted to not show, just to show her that she's right about you. You seem to make a lot of sacrifices to protect her.

HUSBAND: What?

THERAPIST: She thinks that you won't call your boss or show up here next week. (to Wife) Isn't that true?

WIFE: Yeah.

THERAPIST: So you are inclined to act as she expects so she won't have to deal with her part of this little mess. It's your job to take all the blame.

HUSBAND & WIFE: (silence.)

WIFE: What do you mean, my part?

THERAPIST: It looks like you do a lot of worrying about his drinking and his job.

WIFE: Well, I have to.

THERAPIST: Maybe, but if you make his job and his drinking your responsibility, then why should he worry about them? (to Husband) How did you get her to do that?

HUSBAND: What?

THERAPIST: How did you convince her to take responsibility for your job and your drinking?

HUSBAND: I don't know. I wish she'd stop.

WIFE: How can I when you don't take any responsibility?

THERAPIST: Looks like you have a vicious circle here. I have a crazy proposition which may help you break it. Do you want to try it?

HUSBAND: Sure!

WIFE: O.K.

THERAPIST: (to Wife) You have to spend at least fifteen minutes every day bugging him about his boss and his drinking. (to Husband) Your job is to show her it won't work, so when she bugs you, start to drink and keep drinking until she stops. (to Wife) If you bug him enough, he'll never talk to his boss.

WIFE: What good will that do?

THERAPIST: It will help you become more aware of how the two of you get stuck.

HUSBAND: Sounds crazy.

THERAPIST: I told you it was. See if you can make her bug you when she's not planning to. Also, see if you can make her go for more than fifteen minutes. If you can get her to go to half an hour, you don't have to talk to your boss that day. Are you willing to try it?

HUSBAND: O.K.

WIFE: Yeah . . . sure.

THERAPIST: It will be harder than you think. Next week we'll talk about why it is so hard.

The therapist here has very limited goals. These are: (1)

Avoid getting caught in the trap of allying with the wife and confronting the husband; (2) confuse them so they are less sure of themselves and their view of reality; (3) make it harder for them to pursue one dysfunctional sequence (in this case Drink-Nag-Drink-Nag-Drink); (4) make it likely that they will return for another session. Here the therapist has attacked the dutiful wife and defined the husband's not returning as her victory. This, he hopes, will make it harder for the husband to drop out. The wife, though attacked, cannot quit without endangering her moral ascendancy.

The dysfunctional sequence which the therapist prescribed is one which both the husband and the wife agree occurs—they just disagree on the punctuation. The wife punctuates the sequence: Drink-Nag-Drink-Nag, whereas the husband's view is Nag-Drink-Nag-Drink. The therapist has validated both punctuations, giving an active role to both husband and wife. It is obvious that this couple has a long way to go. It is not within the scope of this work to define the entire course of treatment, but it might be useful to give some examples of how some of the key problems already mentioned might be met in the second conjoint interview:

THERAPIST: Hello. How are you folks doing?

HUSBAND: O.K.

WIFE: O.K.

THERAPIST: Great. Did you try the homework?

HUSBAND: Sort of.

THERAPIST: What do you mean?

WIFE: He talked to his boss.

THERAPIST: He did? Did you nag him into it?

WIFE: No. I never mentioned it.

THERAPIST: Really? But that was part of your homework assignment.

WIFE: (Defensively) I never got a chance. Besides, it seemed stupid. Anyway, he talked to his boss the day after we came in here.

THERAPIST: He did? Well, he certainly got you off the hook. (to Husband) You talked to your boss?

HUSBAND: Yeah. (Note the rich expression here.)

THERAPIST: I'm almost afraid to ask you how it went. (Flagrant manipulation. Note that Therapist is not asking a question, only stating that he is almost afraid to ask one. He can back off if necessary without losing face.)

HUSBAND: Not so good. (Note that Husband is responding as if Therapist asked the question.) He's threatening to fire me.

THERAPIST: (Silence.)

HUSBAND: He says I drink on the job.

THERAPIST: He does? (The trap here is to be seen as an ally of the boss.)

HUSBAND: Yeah. (More rich expression. The above query did not produce the hoped-for monologue.)

THERAPIST: What are you going to do now?

HUSBAND: I don't know. (He's not making this easy.)

THERAPIST: Did you tell him that your drinking is none of his business?

HUSBAND: No.

THERAPIST: I'm getting a sense you don't want to discuss this.

HUSBAND: No, it's O.K. He said if he caught me drinking again, he'd fire me.

THERAPIST: Sounds like he's really on your case.

HUSBAND: No, he's right. I have been drinking too much. I've got to cut down. (This is a key point. It is important that Therapist not jump on the bandwagon of reform. There is not enough room for two.)

THERAPIST: What do you mean you've been drinking too much? Don't you have a right to drink as you like? You're over twenty-one.

HUSBAND: I shouldn't drink at work. It slows me down.

THERAPIST: How do you know?

HUSBAND: I just know. I don't work as well when I'm drinking. I'd better not drink at work anymore.

THERAPIST: You know, it's not easy to quit drinking at a time you usually drink. Especially if someone else tells you you should. I'm not sure you can stop, even if you want to.

WIFE: He'd better quit! We can't afford to lose that job.

THERAPIST: Maybe, but I doubt you and his boss can get him to quit if he doesn't want to. Do you think he cares what you think about his drinking? (This attack might seem unwarranted, but Wife is actually sabotaging Husband's process by making her usual statements. He can react against her intrusion by backing off his decision. Therapist must block this.)

THERAPIST: (to Husband) You'd better not quit drinking for your wife or your boss.

HUSBAND: No, I'm quitting for myself.

THERAPIST: For yourself. Why? Don't you like to drink?

HUSBAND: Not really. It's more of a habit at this point.

THERAPIST: A habit? Do you think you're an alcoholic?

HUSBAND: No, I can quit anytime.

THERAPIST: Well, I hope you're right, but I'm not sure it'll be so easy.

HUSBAND: I can do it!

Therapist has avoided the traps here and created a nice flexible position. If Husband stops drinking, Husband wins by outwitting the therapist. If not, the therapist can say "I told you so" and maintain credibility. But there is more to do.

THERAPIST: (to Wife) Think he can do it?

WIFE: No. He's said this before.

THERAPIST: (to Husband) Well, if you do this, you'll have to do it without her faith. Do you mean you won't drink at work or just not get drunk at work?

HUSBAND: I'm not going to drink at all! (Always the high roller.)

THERAPIST: What?

HUSBAND: That's right!

THERAPIST: Why?

HUSBAND: It's not doing me any good. My wife's on my case. My boss is on my case. It's not even him anymore.

THERAPIST: You know that's easy to say and hard to do.

HUSBAND: I know.

THERAPIST: How long do you plan to do this?

HUSBAND: A year. At least.

THERAPIST: Oh, c'mon.

HUSBAND: No, I mean it!

THERAPIST: (to Wife) Think he can do it?

WIFE: Well, if he sets his mind to it. (She avoids the trap.)

THERAPIST: You mean you'll bet he can do it? What do you think the odds are?

WIFE: He does anyway.

THERAPIST: So you don't think he can do it?

WIFE: No.

THERAPIST: Well, I'm not sure you're wrong, but I'm holding my bet for now. (to both) Do you want to meet again?

HUSBAND: Sure.

WIFE: Yes.

THERAPIST: I'll see you a week from today. I wish you good luck, but I'm afraid you may be setting yourselves up. (to Husband) If you don't drink this week, you will be proving your wife wrong, so you can expect her to provide you with plenty of excuses to drink. (to Wife) The danger for you is to feel responsible for his not drinking and to try to tiptoe around him. If you do that, I guarantee he'll manipulate you like crazy. Don't let yourself get tricked into trying to keep him sober against your own interests. As a matter of fact, you might even see if you can get him to drink and see how strong his resolve is. (to Husband) Think she can get you to drink?

HUSBAND: No!

THERAPIST: I'm not so sure. (to Husband) If you drink, at least you can blame her.

WIFE: He does anyway.

HUSBAND: I won't drink, so it won't be a problem!

THERAPIST: Well, good luck to both of you. You'll need it!

This interview demonstrates some responses to the more common traps set by alcoholic couples. The counselor must avoid selling sobriety to the husband or protecting him from the wife. It is also very important that the therapist not invest in the husband's sobriety. By predicting problems, the therapist actually gains credibility if the husband drinks. In fact, Carter Umbarger of the Family Institute of Cambridge once said, "A therapist is always safe in predicting disaster. If the disaster is averted, the clients can feel justly proud of themselves, and if the disaster occurs, at least they know they have a smart therapist."

The other major move the therapist made in this interview was to try to enlist the competitive and resentful feelings of the couple in the cause of recovery. By getting the wife to predict failure, the husband can only show his independence from his wife by not drinking, rather than by drinking and proving her right.

The goal of the therapist at this stage of treatment is to change the way drinking operates in the family system. As the wife loses her job as the voice of temperance, drinking becomes a much less effective way for the husband to declare his independence. Once this occurs, the therapist can work to stop the drinking. There are many ways of doing this—not all as easy as in the previous interview—but a basic tool at the therapist's disposal is the specter of alcoholism.

When any couple is arguing about the drinking of one partner, the therapist can ask the drinking member whether he or she is alcoholic. If the person says yes, then the issue becomes appropriate treatment: A.A., possibly inpatient treatment, possibly Antabuse. After all, the person has just claimed to be suffering from an invariably fatal condition and obviously needs treatment. Any other course can be defined as suicidal.

If, however, the person denies being alcoholic, then the discussion can focus on why the other person objects to the drinking. Even if the objections are quite exaggerated, there is no question that drinking is causing a problem in the relationship, and because the drinking isn't very important to the drinker, it is easy for him to agree to stop or cut down drastically. If the drinker is able to stop drinking dysfunctionally over time, then he gets an opportunity to learn to negotiate the relationship sober; if he cannot, then the question of why he cannot must be addressed.

In general, if people who drink dysfunctionally stop drinking for a significant period of time, it becomes easier for them to see the cost of their drinking. Very often they remain sober in order to avoid having to label themselves "alcoholic."

Once the drinking has stopped, or at least the alcoholic has made stopping a goal, the second stage of treatment begins. One important determinant of how treatment should proceed is whether the alcoholic diagnoses himself as such. If he considers himself to be alcoholic, then the resources of A.A. are brought to bear. In the context of an alcoholic trying to recover, sobriety is such a heavy issue that the priority is to preserve it. This means that working on couple or family issues is suspended except as they directly relate to sobriety. The therapist must watch carefully to determine what form the family homeostatic reaction is taking and then frame it positively and prescribe or predict it. This move should be made with as much of the family present as possible. Apart from this type of move, conjoint therapy should be suspended and the family members insulated from each other as much as possible. The husband should see an alcoholism counselor and the wife should be referred to a female psychotherapist. The children in any case should be referred to groups designed for children of alcoholics. The family or couple can return to cojoint therapy when a return to drinking doesn't seem to be a clear and present danger. When this happens, the danger of relapse should be directly discussed, and a contract stating what everyone will do in the event of relapse must be formally agreed upon.

In the case where the husband has quit drinking but does not diagnose himself as alcoholic, the family therapist in many ways has a much freer hand. Because the husband is defined as a nonalcoholic who is at present choosing not to drink, there is no need to protect him from issues or responsibility. If he does drink again, rather than having to deal with a Break Out, the therapist can just deal with what is communicated by the decision and slowly co-opt the rationalizations until the husband is again forced to choose between stopping or admitting that his drinking is beyond his control and therefore alcoholic in nature.

The therapist can make the same moves against the family's

homeostatic responses whether or not the husband is an admitted alcoholic, but when the drinker is allowed to resist the label of alcoholic, he pays for this privilege by surrendering the protection usually afforded a recovering alcoholic in early sobriety. Therefore he is expected to change his way of functioning as a parent and husband, with the therapist standing ready to predict a return to drinking any time the husband begins to act suspicious. A phrase like "You know, an alchholic under the pressure you're under would break out in a second," can work wonders. With these tools available, a therapist can often move through issues much faster than one might expect. It must be stated here, however, that these tactics tend to be appropriate when the alcoholism has not progressed to obvious chronicity. A man who has repeated detoxifications and long-standing alcoholism in his background will need treatment designed for the chronic alcoholic. So will his family.

As a family logs more and more time living without drunkenness and its related emergency as a focus for their lives, it is forced to develop coping mechanisms which do not depend on sedatives and scapegoating. As this happens, the therapist can shift the focus to secondary dysfunctional strategies, such as competing rather than cooperating as parents, or manipulating rather than stating needs directly. Sometimes by this stage the therapist can point out problems and facilitate a problem-solving process. If this meets with resistance, however, well worn-in tools lie close at hand. A competitive parenting situation might be countered by empowering the children to hand out "parenting points" when either parent meets their favor—with a prize to the "winner," for example. A manipulator can be complimented on technique, with the therapist—a professional manipulator—offering pointers to enhance expertise further.

As time passes the intensity begins to leave the game. The members of the family begin to care more about their own pursuits than scoring points against each other. The closeness of people who have survived a time of mortal danger together begins to replace fusion and enmeshment. As the parents develop a grudging trust for each other, the question of who controls the context becomes less vital. Moments of intimacy begin to occur. This intimacy spreads to the children who, now that they have parents, can stop parenting or trying to force the parents to do their job. All this makes available energy which previously was used for survival in the tight, desperate game— energy which can be used to grow, to learn, to love. The clever analyses of the therapist lose their fascination. Family members no longer are much interested in what the therapist thinks of them. Usually they remember to send a Christmas card.

To Close:

There is an implication in the preceding chapters that therapy with alcoholic families is a fairly simple procedure which usually concludes successfully. This implication is not one I wish completely to disown. It is true that any process of change is fraught with complexities, complications, and disappointments, and that alcoholic families tend to provide a generous supply of surprises and setbacks. It is also true, however, that a therapist who is aware that the process of change must include regression and resistance is able to experience these things not as failure, but as grist for the therapeutic mill.

My wish for this work is that it will go some way toward persuading readers that the process of changing the behavior and attitudes of others is not mysterious or magical, requiring initiation into arcane arts and languages, but a relatively straightforward process which can be accomplished in reasonable time and with a high probability of success by ordinary humans. A therapist who shares the clients' view that they have almost no chance to live, act, and feel differently from the way they have always done is unlikely to be of much help.

A therapist with a clear expectation of success and an understanding that any change is going to be greeted by extreme ambivalence is in a much better position to be of help.

PART II

The Case of
the Dutiful
Daughter

4

Delusions
of Adequacy:
A Failed Therapy

This section will provide the reader with something of the flavor of doing therapy with an alcoholic family. The idea was derived from a case in which I seriously botched the treatment and then was given a second chance. I hoped to show the contrast between the work I did as a beginning family therapist with work done when I was considerably more experienced. As I wrote, however, I found that the case as it actually occurred did not allow me to make all the points I wished to make. As the tension between literature and history mounted, I finally made a clear choice for fictionalization.

There is no "real" Cristie family. The personalities of each member are composites of several members of different families, and the treatment, though based on notes and tapes, is also a composite of the treatments of several families. Moreover, this account of treatment has more clarity of technique than I am usually able to accomplish in real life.

However, while "The Case of the Dutiful Daughter" may not be historically accurate, to the best of my ability it is emotionally and clinically authentic. Everything that took place with the Cristies has happened in my practice in one way or another. I hope I have communicated to the reader the subjective experience of applying the treatment approach outlined in the first part of the book.

Diana had not called for an appointment nor did she come by a professional referral. She said that a friend had given her my name and said I was "OK for a shrink." Diana made herself at home immediately. Sprawling in a comfortably worn easy chair, she began rattling off her history with the ease of long practice.

Some of the facts escaped me, however, because I was rather distracted by Diana herself. She was fifteen years old and looked two years older. She wore shorts and a halter and had clearly done some serious work on her tan. Her blue eyes were in striking contrast to her deep tan and jet black hair. Her fresh energetic clean-cut appearance and humorous articulate presentation were in equally sharp contrast to the story she was relating with girlish charm.

Diana had just gone AWOL from a Therapeutic Community which she had voluntarily entered for drug treatment two weeks earlier. She left because they were going to shave her head as a punishment for putting dishes away wet.

I asked her why she had entered the T.C. in the first place. She answered that her drug problem had scared her and that she had "lost it" on "acid" (LSD) just before checking into the treatment program. She also reported using large quantities of marijuana, pills, and alcohol. I asked her if she had ever used heroin and she said her boyfriend had offered it to her, but she had refused. There was a clear implication of "so far."

I then asked about her boyfriend. Diana replied that he "isn't really my boyfriend, just a guy I hang out with. I'm not in love with him or anything." She went on to report that Billy was twenty years old, worked part-time in an auto parts store and was really into wine. She did, however, leave the impression that Billy also indulged in several other psychoactive medications.

Diana didn't mind Billy's drinking because it made him "less horny." I asked if he was pressuring her sexually. She sat motionless for about a minute and then blurted out, "I feel so guilty it's killing me. If my parents ever found out I had sex with Billy, they would die. I never told anyone before. Promise you'll never tell anyone."

I reassured her and asked her about the circumstances. Diana related that Billy wanted sex so much and once when she was "really stoned," she gave in. She claimed not to enjoy sex that much and seemed to feel guilty and embarrassed in talking about it. I asked her if she had used birth control; she said she hadn't. I asked her what she would do if she got pregnant. She said she didn't know, but she didn't believe in abortion. I then asked her what she would do if Billy pressured her again. Again she said she didn't know.

At this point I treated her to a few inspirational remarks about birth control and standing up for herself. She listened politely, then asked if I had ever done drugs.

My reply began hesitantly, but soon accelerated to a rather romanticized account of my life on the street and my early career as a jazz musician. It made a rollicking yarn, factually accurate but somewhat embellished. I even managed to work in a reference to my motorcycle parked outside the office.

Diana seemed impressed and said that she thought I could help her.

"If you're going to see me, you can't use drugs," I said sternly.

"Can you make a promise not to use any drugs while I am treating you?"

She solemnly promised, and we made an appointment for later that week. At her next appointment Diana was dressed less provocatively. She was staying off drugs and had not seen Billy. She thought that avoiding both would be easier once school had started. When I asked her about school, she reported doing honor-roll work in spite of the fact she was "stoned ninety-nine percent of the time."

The rest of the session was spent on her family. She was a middle child with an older sister eighteen and a younger sister aged ten. Her father was a middle-level executive in a large insurance company whom she described as an "uptight asshole." Her mother was "angry all the time" and had never worked outside the home. Diana didn't feel close to anyone in her family except her younger sister, who was "cute and quiet." Her older sister was entering her second year of nursing school and was a "know-it-all goody-good," although Diana couldn't understand how such a "fat bitch" could land a boyfriend like Sal.

She said her parents didn't like the idea of her coming to see me and wanted her to go to a psychiatrist, but she had told them that the only treatment she would accept was from me (she would run away if they tried to make her see a psychiatrist). According to Diana, I was the only decent counselor she had ever seen.

She asked if I thought she should complain to the police because her father had slapped her face and had struck her on previous occasions. Her mother hit her, too, but then would get all "guilty and weepy," Diana claimed. Her father cared only about controlling her and hit her whenever she tried to stand up for herself; she hated and feared him, she said.

Through all this I was extremely sympathetic. Diana's loneliness, confusion, and sensitivity were eloquently and poignantly expressed. I, too, had been misunderstood, bullied, and made to feel guilty by my parents during my teenage years. I, too, had used drugs as a way of coping. It was easy to empathize with Diana's situation.

Diana, sensitive and perceptive as she was, sensed this. In making it clear that I was the best counselor she had ever met, she provided detailed satiric descriptions of other counselors who had tried to help her. I, of course, honoring the ethics of my craft, forbore to agree with her openly. On the other hand, it is difficult for me to recall any arguments we had on the subject of colleagues. And Diana, meanwhile, hung on my every word, laughed at my jokes, agreed enthusiastically with my insights and interpretations, and also avoided drugs and Billy.

Despite this rosy situation, a few aspects of what was transpiring caused me concern. Apart from keeping two counseling appointments a week, Diana seemed to have no activities or interests. She had given up her major activities—drugs and Billy—but had replaced them with nothing. She seemed to have no close friends who were not heavily drug-involved or much older. She did not spend time with family members, although she seemed to feel sympathetic and protective toward her younger sister. It was difficult to get a clear picture of how she spent her time.

As a former English teacher I tried to give Diana books by authors I thought she might like—J. P. Donleavy, Kingsley Amis, for instance. Of course, she did not read them, but she felt guilty about *not* reading them, having correctly perceived that I was invested in improving her mind.

I might also have given Diana the books to provide us with something to talk about, for I was finding it difficult to fill two sessions a week. Early sessions dealt with "war stories," but these began to wear thin. I was also hesitant about glorifying the behavior I was trying to change. Naturally I delved into her feelings. She found it easy to experience and express anger and frustration toward her parents; boredom, loneliness and despair about her life; caring and concern toward her younger sister. Once these feelings were expressed and discussed, however, I didn't have much idea what to do with them. What confidence I felt at the beginning of the process was starting to erode.

My work at the agency was supervised by a psychiatrist who was smart, experienced, and tough. My discomfort with Diana had gone on for several weeks, however, before I saw fit to bring up this aspect of the therapy. Up to then I was confidently reporting good progress and giving the impression that I felt more objective and in charge than was the case. For instance, I did not report occasionally finding myself welcoming sessions on warm sunny days when Diana would show up in abbreviated attire.

In any event, when I finally revealed that I was not as comfortable or sanguine as I once had been in my treatment of

Diana, our consultant was able to hide whatever shock he might have felt. He explained that her emptiness and despair, her anger at parents and previous counselors, and her needy dependence on me indicated that she might be suffering from a "borderline personality." He added that it would be a good idea to limit my emotional involvement with her (where did he get that idea?) and also to set limits on her in our relationship. Even then I think I was able to appreciate the gentleness with which this psychiatrist handled me. He warned me off my obvious induction without embarrassing me in front of a staff for which I was responsible.

His perceptions, however, were limited by his assumption that Diana's problems existed within her and were only superficially and tangentially connected to those around her. Therefore, although he was able to warn me away from possible disaster, he had no more idea than I how to make Diana better. The prognosis for successful treatment of the "borderline personality" is not optimistic. (Many years later a friend who was a traditionally trained psychiatrist jokingly remarked that he had found that the best treatment for the "borderline personality" was to refer these patients to other therapists, preferably those who had in some way incurred his hostility.)

At our next session Diana could sense a change immediately and asked what was wrong. "You seem real uptight. You remind me of my dad or something!" (The ultimate putdown.) I maintained my professional stance and pushed harder to get her involved in activities where she could meet other young people who were not marinated in chemicals. She seemed bored and distant. I probably could have achieved an identical response by lecturing on the prevalence of iambic meters in Elizabethan poetry.

I might stop here and offer the reader a one-question quiz: What is going to happen now? As I collect the papers, I see that everyone has answered correctly. Indeed, Diana missed the next session without calling to cancel (a first) and showed up for the following session in extreme disrepair. The formerly glowing skin was grubby and unhealthy-looking, her eyes dull and unfocused, her face slack and shadowed.

"What are you on?" I asked.

"Nothing," she said.

"Nothing? You look like the poster girl for *The Drug Menace.*"

"I'm all right," she maintained. "Besides, what do you care?"

"Why the hell should I care more about you than you do?"

"You're just like everyone else," Diana said. "You say you care about me, and the second I do something you don't like, you're all over my case."

"I'm on your case because I care about you," I countered.

"That's exactly what my dad says." Check.

"How did you get here?" I asked, attempting a diversion.

"Billy drove me." Check.

"I thought you weren't seeing Billy," I said.

"It doesn't matter anyway," Diana said, managing to look even sadder. "I can't see you anymore because I took drugs." Checkmate.

I remembered the rule I had smugly pronounced just five weeks earlier. I had set a rule and she had broken it. If I ignored that, my credibility was nil. On the other hand, dropping her as a patient was inconceivable. Even if I could reconcile this to myself, it was hard to see how a drug counselor would refuse to treat someone because that person showed evidence of a drug problem.

As I began to recover, I realized this debacle might be a blessing in disguise. The therapy with Diana had not been going well before our current impasse. Even if I somehow were able to reinstate my "no drugs" rule and so continue with individual treatment of Diana, it was conceivable that we would be in for a series of scenes like this one. I had no way to stop her from taking drugs, and so far our relationship showed no signs of filling the great emptiness inside her.

I had been reading *Conjoint Family Therapy* by Virginia

Satir, and its step-by-step cookbook format made a lot of sense to me. As Diana eyed me speculatively, I said, "I told you that you couldn't take drugs if you wanted me to treat you, and your condition shows me that you don't want me to treat you. It's obvious you need help, but from now on I'll only see you with your whole family."

A look of panic came into her eyes, then was replaced by rage. "You're fuckin' crazy," she shrieked, the Seconal fuzz disappearing from her voice. "I don't want them in here! I hate them! I thought you cared about me."

As the tirade went on, I found my old confidence returning. Some color seemed to be returning to Diana's cheeks as well. Screaming is good for the circulation.

Finally Diana wound down, and her towering pique deteriorated into a pout. "Besides, they'll never come," she finished lamely.

"That's possible." I said. "Is your mother home now?"

"I don't know."

"May I call her and find out?"

She nodded numbly, and I dialed the phone. After three rings a woman's thin, tense voice answered.

I introduced myself as a counslor who had been seeing Diana and said that I thought it would help her treatment if the family would join the sessions. I also said that Diana seemed to doubt that they would come. With a note of anger in her voice, the mother said she would be happy to come. She would talk to her husband and was sure that he would do anything to help Diana, as would her sisters. "There is only one person in this family who doesn't care about people," she closed.

After hanging up the phone, I asked Diana whether she would be willing to attend.

"I'll think about it," she snapped. Suddenly she seemed very young and genuinely disconcerted by this turn of events. The session ended soon after. I tried to catch a glimpse of Billy as his car noisily disappeared but caught only a vague silhouette. The mother called later to say that her husband had agreed

to come, and we made an appointment for an evening that
week.

The Cristie family radiated middle-class respectability. Their
clothes seemed particularly new and fashionable in contrast
with the Salvation Army–modern decor of my agency. They
seemed ill at ease but determinedly cheerful.

Charles, Diana's father, was a tall, spare, military-looking
man with a gray crew cut and a gray three-piece suit. He had
arranged his rock-jawed, youthful face into a convincing smile,
but his gray eyes were uncomfortably penetrating. He had a
good handshake.

Paula Cristie, Diana's mother, was also spare and well
dressed, in a brown tweed suit. Her mouth was tight and heavily lined, and although she, too, was smiling, I imagined that
she was suffering from a headache. She shook my hand quickly
and then perched at the edge of a wooden chair.

Martha, Diana's older sister, looked older than her eighteen
years. Neatly dressed in dark wool slacks and a green sweater,
she was neither as fat nor as unattractive as her sister had led
me to believe. She wore neither makeup nor smile but did
shake my hand as she introduced herself.

Tina was almost eleven but looked more like eight. She lacked
the strong features of her two sisters and showed her mother's
nervous quality without her mother's air of strength and discipline. Apparently very shy, she gave the impression of cling-
ing to her mother's skirt although she was not actually touching
her. She wore jeans and a T-shirt with a "smile face."

"Is that the only smile I'm going to get from you?" I asked,
pointing at her shirt. She was not amused.

Diana herself, in contrast to our last meeting, looked healthy,
alert, and relaxed, in spotless white jeans and a crisply ironed
shirt. She moved about the room with a proprietary air, pointing out the limited points of interest the agency had to offer,
and warned her mother away from a chair with a collapsed
bottom.

When everyone was finally settled, I asked if they all knew why they were here. Every face turned toward Mother, who spoke immediately. "We came to help Diana get off drugs."

I asked if that was why everyone was here. No one changed expression. I asked Paula how she had found out about Diana's drug use. She said that Diana had told her that she had tried marijuana when she was eleven and at twelve was sent home from school because she "looked funny." At that time she had admitted to taking "some pills" and was rushed to the hospital emergency room where vomiting was induced. The contents of her stomach revealed a small assortment of barbiturates and amphetamines. Diana had been sent to a psychiatrist who treated her for a year. Paula Cristie said that she had talked to the psychiatrist two or three times over the course of the year and that he had been vague about what was wrong with Diana or what could be done. When Diana had become more and more resistant, Paula had let her terminate therapy. The psychiatrist had been expensive and had seemed to do no good; about three months after having treatment, Diana overdosed. This time her stomach was pumped, producing a somewhat larger assortment of barbiturates and amphetamines—a dose that was not potentially fatal but disturbing. It was not reassuring to remember Diana's story that she had intentionally overdosed because her father had beaten her.

I asked Charles if he had beaten Diana. He smiled quickly and said that he had slapped her for being disrespectful the day before the incident. He had felt terrible about this after the overdose but said he had only slapped her once and she had deserved it.

"Bullshit!" Diana shouted. "You're always hitting us. I think you enjoy it. If you felt bad, why didn't you stop?"

Things were moving faster than I had planned. I knew whatever I did next was likely to be important and searched for an appropriate strategy.

Mother came to the rescue. "Diana is so provocative, it's a wonder anyone can keep their temper around her; I admit I sometimes slap her, too."

"You don't hit me the way he does. It's not the same," Diana said.

Martha, the older sister, jumped in. "You're always talking about how people treat *you*—how about thinking about how you treat people? You don't care about the pain and suffering you cause. You always blame everyone else for your troubles!"

"Fuck you!" Diana nimbly retorted.

"I don't cause *you* any pain—you don't give a shit about me anyway." Martha didn't look up, but her voice was intense. "Mom and Dad bend over backwards to help you and you spit in their faces. Don't you think they're tired of running around to drug places 'cause you keep screwing up?"

"Stop it, both of you," their mother said in a tired voice.

I looked at Charles but couldn't gauge his expression. He was leaning over staring at the rug, supporting himself with his forearms on his knees. Tina, the younger daughter, sat motionless. I had the fantasy that she was trying to become invisible. She saw me looking at her and looked down, blushing.

"You were telling me that Diana had taken an overdose last year and that they pumped her stomach," I reminded Paula. "What happened then?"

"We tried to get her to go back to the psychiatrist, and she wouldn't go," Paula said, "but she agreed to see a drug counselor in one of those drop-in centers. She seemed to be doing all right until she got arrested."

Diana had told me about this arrest, but I feigned surprise in order to protect her confidentiality. "Arrested?" I asked.

"Yes, she was in a car with some friends, and they were pretty wild. The police stopped them and found some pills and marijuana joints in her purse. They called me to come down and get her. I never thought I would see my own daughter in jail! Charlie knew the judge, so when we went to court, they continued her case for six months. Afterward we told Diana that she had to get help and go to a drug program. I got her into Project Rebirth. She stayed ten days and ran away. She said they were going to cut off her hair, but they told me they had just refused to let her call her boyfriend. Diana insists that they are lying. I don't know what to believe, but Diana said she would run away from home if we made her go back. Then she found you, and she seemed much happier. We are all so grateful and ready to do anything to help.''

Paula seemed to sense that the family needed her to keep talking.

"It's been a nightmare. Diana was always such a lively, talented girl, always popular and did so well in school. I can't understand how this drug thing happened. If it weren't for drugs . . . I know girls Diana's age who get involved with sex, but Diana has always been so good about that and confided in me—just like Martha.''

I thought I saw a slight smile on Diana's face. When I turned fully to look at her, however, she was staring blankly into space.

"We love Diana,'' Paula continued, "and we will do anything we have to do to get her back again.'' The more wound-up Paula became, the more leaden and enervated everyone else became. I realized that I was not immune to this dynamic; when she finished talking, I had joined the ranks of stonefaces in the room. Glancing around, Paula Cristie seemed to become still more agitated. I wondered if she was paralyzing everyone else or if the paralysis of the others was making her more agitated, or both. It was obvious that she was going to speak again unless someone intervened. I spoke.

"I wonder whether you have something to add, Mr. Cristie?'' I asked.

He seemed shocked to have been addressed. Although he changed position and was now looking at me, the glazed, entranced look remained on his face. "Uh . . . Yeah . . . We . . . We've been very concerned about Diana for a long time. She's a great kid, but she keeps getting involved with those drugs. I tried to talk to her, but it just winds up in an argument. I feel bad because I wasn't around enough when she was little. I work long hours and left the kids pretty much up to Paula. Martha didn't seem to have any trouble. She got good grades, got elected to Student Council, and made class secretary her senior year. She's doing well in nursing school and is getting engaged this spring. Diana seemed to be doing well, too. Even when she started having problems, no one could believe it. Everyone thought it was a mistake. Even now she still does well in school, she doesn't lie or steal, and she's a good girl, if you know what I mean. She *knows* how dangerous the drugs are and says she wants to stop, but something inside her seems to make her go back to them over and over. It's like a sickness." He trailed off, looking dazed, and gazed at me expectantly.

"Everyone here is concerned for Diana," I began. "She has had overdoses and arrests and what not, and we all know that she needs help. But Diana is just expressing the family's pain," I said, calling on Virginia Satir. "She is expressing a family problem, and if the whole family works on it, I think we can solve it."

"What do you mean expressing the family's pain?" Martha asked. "She *is* the family's pain. Things would be fine if she would just realize that the feelings of others are more important than her cheap thrills!"

"I'm not sure what you mean by a family problem," Mrs. Cristie said. "Diana is a problem for all of us, but only she can solve it. If you could tell me what I'm doing wrong, I'll do everything in my power to change, but right now Diana is the problem in this family, and the family has done all it knows how to do to help her."

Diana's father remained in trance. Feeling less intimidated by the minute, I noted that the session was at an end. We made an appointment for the following week, and the family filed out. Diana gave me a reassuring smile, and as little Tina passed, I thought I saw a tear in her eye. I realized that she had not said a word during the session and I had scarcely noticed her.

I began to review my reactions. It was clear that the picture of the family I had inferred from Diana's descriptions clashed dramatically with what I had observed. I had been expecting

Paula to be mousy, tentative, and reticent and Charles to be an officer type. I had no idea what had precipitated Charles's near-total collapse, but Paula seemed able to fill the void. I found myself feeling positively toward Charles. Even at that time I suspected that my reaction might be partially due to gratitude. I had expected him to be cold, powerful, and disapproving. Instead he was passive, compliant, and depressed, and I was somewhat ashamed to acknowledge the relief I felt.

Martha seemed to be the voice of anger for the family, the one who felt the need to sweep in and save the parents from Diana's abuse. It was hard to experience Paula Cristie as someone who needed protection, but perhaps Martha knew something that I didn't. As I thought about Martha, I realized that I didn't much like her. There seemed to be no good reason for this reaction; she was bright, articulate, and attractive. I began to suspect that my mild antipathy toward her was due to her attacks on Diana, my baby.

I realized I felt a mild antipathy toward little Tina as well. I attributed it to the fact that she had reacted to me somewhat as though I were a houseplant. I had just as scrupulously ignored her. That showed her!

Diana, too, had behaved very differently from what I had expected—all the more disturbing in her case because my expectations had been formed from personal experience rather than hearsay. I had expected real anger toward me—both for my withdrawal from our individual relationship and for my bringing her family into treatment. But the jealous brat side of Diana did not make an appearance. She did not seem to feel betrayed or deprived. With some chagrin, I found myself asking myself, doesn't she care enough about me to punish me for leaving her?

According to Fred Duhl, "Technique is what you use until the therapist shows up." Having a week to ponder a problem has advantages and disadvantages. There is plenty of time to think of solutions, but there is also plenty of time to second-guess those solutions and drive oneself crazy. In any case, I now decided to come at the family from an angle they didn't expect. As I found out in later practice, it is often a good idea to keep families off-balance and confused. It upsets their usual procedure for regulating the impact an outsider can have upon them. I thought I would employ a family-therapy technique called family sculpture.

This is a potentially powerful technique derived from psychodrama. It allows a family member to represent his or her experience in the family in the language of space and movement. The family member who is the "sculptor" physically guides other family members to adopt positions, gestures, and movements that metaphorically express the feeling of the family from the sculptor's unique point of view. One of the advantages of this technique is that the physical expressing of a situation often carries an emotional power that might be lost in a verbal description (particularly if the sculptor has limited verbal ability). In addition, it is much more difficult to dissemble in an unfamiliar language. Information may be revealed by family sculpture which might never come out verbally.

I had decided to ask the silent daughter Tina to sculpt the family, on the hunch that someone who has the power to become invisible must see a lot. It was a high-risk plan; so far as I could see, I had no rapport with Tina. If she refused to cooperate, or if the technique went nowhere, I would feel even more incompetent with this family.

The Cristies arrived on time. Greetings were perfunctory, and it was clear that everyone was upset. Diana seemed in high outrage. The set of Paula's jaw alone was sufficient to express her mood. Charles seemed stunned and dejected, though resplendent in a tweed three-piece suit. Martha and Tina were hard to read.

"How is everybody?" I asked.

"Why don't you tell him, Diana?" Paula said, fixing her daughter with a glare so intense that I almost expected the plant behind Diana's head to wither.

"*You* tell him," Diana said, returning the glare.

"Diana got sent home from school today," said Paula. "They thought she was high on something."

"Bullshit!" Diana shot back. "That bitch Mrs. Ryan is always looking for something to bust me for."

"You expect us to believe you after all that's happened?" Charles asked.

And off they went, with mother attacking, Diana defending, and father occasionally putting in his two-cents worth (a generous assessment). There were two major harangues from Martha, both when her mother cried. Tina kept her own counsel, but her eyes darted from speaker to speaker as if she were watching a tennis match.

As Diana treated her mother to considerable feedback concerning her character and parenting skills, she seemed to be getting the upper hand. Paula, so formidable at first, was wilting. When Charles tried to intervene, he was ignored by both Diana and her mother. Diana scored solidly, as when she said, "You don't care what happens to me as long as your precious bridge club doesn't find out (satiric nasal voice). Mrs. Cristie, your daughter is dead (satiric haughty voice)."

After a half hour of this, I realized that the sculpture with Tina would not be the order of the day, but I had to do something. I decided to capitalize on my relationship with Diana and try to calm her down. Charles had just asked Diana for the third time why she was so unhappy. I cut him off.

"Diana," I said firmly, "I've been listening to this for a long time, and I still can't figure out what happened. Today was only your second day in school, right?" She nodded.

"What period was it when you were sent home?"

"Homeroom," she said in a subdued, little-girl voice.

After a bit of prodding, Diana did admit to smoking one joint before homeroom. It also turned out that she had not heard her homeroom teacher ask her a question several times. That had provoked a giggling fit, after which Diana was sent to the nurse's office and then home. During this exchange, the other family members were silent.

The interview ended with Diana's promise that she would

not use drugs before or during school. Paula thanked me warmly as she left, and Charles looked grateful as he limply shook my hand. The three girls filed out in silence.

The next session also went well. I had been anticipating it all week, and what I perceived to be my newfound credibility gave me the energy and determination to convince a reluctant Tina to try a family sculpture. Once the procedure started, she began to thrive in the role of telling family members where to go and what to do. She would give someone a pose, then back up and examine it the way a sculptor might examine a work in progress, then ask for a slight change or correction, stepping back again to note the effect. Unlike many children, she was able to grasp the concept of metaphor immediately. She did not attempt to make a literal sculpture of the family at a dinner table or in the living room (Mommy sits there with Daddy at the head of the table) but lined the family up as she felt them to be.

She placed her mother in the center of the room flanked by Martha and Diana. Martha faced mother and Diana faced away, but glancing back frequently. She placed herself behind this triangle at an angle between Diana and mother. When I asked Tina to give herself a gesture, she thought a moment and then snapped into the catatonic pose that had seemed her entire repertoire before this session.

Almost as an afterthought, she placed Charles as far away from the group as the limited space allowed. When asked what she would like changed in the family, she said that she wanted Diana and her mother to stop fighting, for Martha to talk to her more, and for her father to do things with her.

I asked Charles if he was surprised at his placement. He said he was, that he didn't feel as out of the family as Tina had placed him.

"I don't see why not," snapped his wife. "You've never been around for me or anyone else. If Diana had a father, she probably wouldn't be in all this trouble."

Looking miserable, Charles merely said, "I spend time with the kids. I hardly go out anymore."

This was ignored by all. Paula Cristie began to reload, and Tina, our sculptor, retreated into never-never land.

"Charles has never been in this family," Paula told me. "He was an officer in Naval Intelligence when I met him, and all his work was secret. After our marriage we moved from base to base, and he would spend all his time drinking at the officers' club while I sat home. I hoped it would change when Martha was born, but it didn't. When Diana came along, it was worse. My husband would go right from work to the officers' club and drink all night. I was so mad and lonely that I would start fights with him just to have an adult to talk to. It wasn't the drinking that bothered me so much, it was his wanting to spend his time with his buddies, and I didn't even have any friends." She began to cry. Diana was filling up, too. Martha said, "Things are better now. Dad's home a lot more."

"That's true," Paula conceded, "but he still spends all his time in the den watching T.V. and drinking."

"He doesn't drink that much," Martha said. I looked over at the subject of this third-person conversation. Wearing his abstracted, hangdog expression, Charles seemed to be unaffected by the proceedings.

"Maybe not. Maybe I'm oversensitive," said Paula. "Every time I smell liquor on his breath, I think of all those navy camps and all that loneliness. I'm not saying that Charles is a drunk," she said, turning to me. "He goes to work every day and doesn't fall down or beat us up or anything; it's just that I wish he talked to me more."

"I talk to you," said Charles, "but every time I talk to you, I get criticized." I realized that it was odd to hear Charles speak without having been asked a direct question. "Besides," continued Charles, "I'm home much more now. You make me sound like an alcoholic. I don't drink that much, and I keep it under control."

"You might as well be an alcoholic for all I see of you," returned Paula.

"You *are* an alcoholic," said Diana. "You drink all the time, and you hit me."

"He doesn't hit you enough," Martha offered. "If he did, maybe you wouldn't be such a spoiled brat."

"Fuck you," was Diana's ritual reply.

"Charles," I said quickly, "Paula said you didn't spend much time with the kids. Is that true?"

"I guess so," Charles admitted. "I'm vice-president in charge of investigation at Casualty Insurance. I'm responsible for the work of over fifty people. If you want to get ahead in my company, you've got to work long hours. When I get home, I just want to relax. I like to have a few drinks, but it's not a problem."

"I wonder if you could plan to do something with your daughters this week?" I asked.

"Well . . . sure. I'd like that."

"Do you have an idea what you would like to do?"

"I'll have to think about that," fended Charles.

"Do you girls have any suggestions?" I asked.

"He could take us shopping," Diana said.

"Can't you stop being greedy for one second?" Martha asked.

"Fuck you," Diana said again.

"I'm getting tired of your language, young lady," Paula said sternly.

"Well, she's always all over my case, the ass-kissing bitch," Diana said, shoving more chips into the pot.

Paula said, "Diana!" at the same time that Charles said, "Watch your dirty mouth!" Everyone looked at Charles.

"Well, I guess you can come up with a plan for homework," I said quickly. "I'll see you all next week."

A more experienced family therapist might have found in this session all the data necessary to design an effective strategy of intervention. Unfortunately for the Cristie family, at this stage in my career, I had no idea what had happened.

My mind was focused on ways of getting Charles to be more of a father and of stopping the ugly bickering between the older girls. I had felt a desire to protect Diana from Martha's onslaughts. Only later did I think about Tina. Her brief animation had ended when the action started, and she had quickly left the session, leaving her body hostage. Paula's anger had been impressive. I found myself sympathizing with Charles's retreat and realized that I had suggested that Charles do something with his daughters rather than with the family. Obviously I was protecting Charles from his wife.

The next session began with an uncomfortable silence which seemed much longer than the five minutes which ticked by on my watch before I turned to Charles and asked, "What did you do with the girls this week?"

"Um . . . ah, I wasn't able to do it this week." Charles averted his eyes.

"How come?" I asked.

"Well, I was very busy, and so were they," he said, continuing to look like a schoolboy caught without his homework.

"So you girls were busy, too?" I asked.

"Not really," Diana said. "I knew he wouldn't do it. He hasn't done anything with us for years. I wasn't looking forward to it anyway. We would all be uptight."

Martha, as usual, was hot on Diana's heels. "I thought of reminding Dad, but I didn't particularly want to watch Diana twist him around her finger. It's bad enough we have to come here every week because of her. She says this is a waste of time, and I'm beginning to agree."

"I think Diana has been much better since she came here," Paula said. "I think these meetings will do us all good."

I realized that I was feeling somewhat threatened by Martha's vote of no confidence, but Paula's support—for some reason I didn't understand—didn't make me feel better. I turned to Tina. "Were you disappointed by not going with Daddy?"

"I don't know," she said, not making eye contact. Her tone and posture did not invite further questioning. I turned back to Dad.

"Do you think it's a good idea to plan something for next week?" I asked.

"Well, sure . . . actually I'm not so sure the girls want to, and I've been very busy."

"Yeah, busy drinking highballs in the den," Diana said.

"Show some respect, Diana," Paula said.

I looked at Martha and thought I caught the hint of a smile. This was supposed to be her job, attacking Diana after Diana attacked her father. I didn't know it then, but this was the moment when I began to think like a family therapist. Unfortunately, I didn't know what to do with the pattern of interaction I had just perceived, so I simply plunged into the thankless task of coercing Charles to plan an outing with his daughters. Finally it was agreed that he would take them all out to dinner and perhaps a show that Friday night.

Paula canceled the next session, citing her own illness as the reason. She assured me that Diana was doing just fine.

The following week the Cristies arrived looking tense. Immediately I suspected that Diana was on something. She was dressed neatly, but her face was blank and seemed to lag a second or two behind events. Martha set the tone for the session. "My boyfriend, Sal, saw Diana cutting school today and hanging around the Sonoco station with her junkie friends. These meetings aren't doing anything. I'm not coming anymore."

"You're lying," slurred Diana. "Sal wouldn't rat on me even if he saw me, which he didn't."

"Were you in school today?" asked Paula.

"Of course," Diana answered.

"Did you stay all day?" asked Martha.

"Don't you cross-examine me, you're not my mother. Do I go blabbing when I see what you and Sal are doing in his station wagon?"

"Diana!" snapped Paula.

"Don't you start on me either," Diana flashed. "I'm up to here with your shit. I do better in school than she does, so don't get on my face!"

"Don't talk to your mother like that!" Charles said in a loud voice.

"Don't talk to your mother like that!" Diana mimicked in a nasal falsetto. "Should I talk to her the way you talk to her? Huh?!"

"Watch your mouth, or I'll slap your face," Charles said.

"Go ahead! Hit me! I hope it gives you a cheap thrill!"

"O.K., folks, let's calm down. This isn't helping," I said, and amazingly everyone calmed down. Diana slumped in her chair, transformed from provocative fury to sullen righteousness. Charles glared at her for a moment and then reverted to his hangdog posture with his forearms on his knees and his head down. Paula and Martha looked at me expectantly. Tina's posture seemed autistic.

"You're being pretty provocative, Diana," I began. I chose not to mention my suspicion that her behavior was chemically augmented. "Did you, in fact, take off from school today?"

"Only in the afternoon," she admitted.

Once again I treated Charles and Paula to a demonstration of "how to talk to a troubled teenager." I was patient but firm. Diana was sullen but compliant. Never, however, did I ask her about drugs. This was a conscious decision. I didn't want to lose my alliance with her by betraying her in front of her parents—not to mention Martha. I wound up a half hour of intimate discussion with Diana by observing that she would have better luck with her parents if she didn't modify every other noun with fuckin'. She agreed. Everyone seemed much calmer. Even Paula was using all of the seat of her wooden chair. I turned to Charles and asked, "How was the dinner with the girls you planned last session?"

As immediate as it was unexpected, the tension returned. It filled the air like a gas. I felt anxious. There was a prolonged silence. Finally Charles said, "It didn't go too well."

I hoped that this was the opening sentence of a paragraph, but it was followed by another long silence. "It didn't go too well?" I ventured at last.

Still another silence. "I sort of spoiled it," Charles said.

"He got shitfaced and cracked up the car," Diana said.

"There you go with your smart mouth," Martha said, but I felt her heart wasn't in it.

"I had had a hard day at the office," Charles went on, "and I was kind of tense about the evening, so I had a couple too many drinks before I left. When I got to the restaurant, I bumped another car in the parking lot. It was just a little bump, but it shook me up. In the restaurant everyone was tense, and Diana and Martha were bickering. I went to the john and on the way back I stopped at the bar, ordered a double, and took another back to the table. I was feeling a little better, and we had a pretty nice dinner.'' He looked quickly at Diana and Martha for confirmation. Both of them stared straight ahead. He continued. ''We decided to go to a show after dinner. When I tried to get out of the parking lot, I sideswiped a car. That shook me up again, so I missed the driveway and went over the curb and a guy leaned on his horn because he thought I was going to come out in front of him. And then I cut the wheel fast and broke the headlight on a telephone pole. Martha said that she thought she had better drive. I agreed and we went right home.'' Another long silence.

Finally Diana said, ''He had two more drinks at dinner.''

''They were only singles, not doubles,'' Charles said.

Something was beginning to dawn on me. ''Has anything like this happened before?'' I asked. Silence.

''I don't let Charles drive when we go out,'' Paula said wearily. ''I was worried last Friday when he took the girls because I knew he had been drinking, but I thought he would be all right with his daughters along.'' Another pause. ''You can't say anything to him when he's drinking anyway.''

''Do you think you have a drinking problem, Charles?'' I asked.

''I know that I sometimes drink too much, but that's very rare. I use it to relax, and I like the taste of good scotch, but I can control it. Besides, I drink much less than I did when I was in the navy.''

Nobody met my eye as I looked around the room. ''Your kids could have gotten hurt that night,'' I said.

''I know, but I was tired and under a lot of strain. I knew I wasn't O.K. to drive, and I asked Martha to drive.'' Martha looked truly miserable. For the first time I experienced her as a person rather than Diana's nemesis.

''Do you drink every night?'' I pursued.

''Most every night,'' he admitted. ''I usually have a highball before dinner and a couple of drinks while I watch T.V.''

"A couple meaning ten," Diana said. "I count."

"Now, Diana," said Charles in a reasonable tone, "that's simply not true."

"I've worried about his drinking since we were married," Paula said. "My father drank. His brother died on skid row. My father had to have half his stomach taken out. That stopped him. I'm afraid Charles is getting worse." Her voice was flat.

"You're oversensitive," Charles countered, "and I don't blame you, but I don't drink like your father. I can take it or leave it."

"Charles, have you ever been to an A.A. meeting?" I asked.

"You think I'm an alcoholic?"

"Yes."

"You're mistaken. I appreciate your concern, and I know I've been causing everyone a lot of concern. I think it's time I cut down." His tone was now strong and reasonable; he was looking me in the eye, sitting upright. I scanned the room again. The tension had dissipated. Even Tina seemed relieved.

"What do you mean cut down?" I asked.

"I'll have a drink before dinner to unwind and maybe one weak highball while I watch T.V.," he said.

"What if you can't hold it to that?" I said.

"I will," he said confidently.

I believed Charles as he sat there erect and dapper in his suit. We had run fifteen minutes past the end of the session. The family filed out looking like a sports team with a lead after a tough first half. Charles led them out with martial bearing.

I was somewhat dazed as I prepared to close up the agency. Although I felt very good about my work both in calming Diana down and confronting Charles, I was apprehensive. The confidence I usually felt after a good session refused to come into focus.

The next week the Cristies seemed like a different family. Gone was Charles's hangdog look. Paula was still tense, but she wore a brave smile. Diana and Martha were talking about clothes as if they were the best of friends. Even Tina granted me an eighth of a smile when I greeted her.

"Diana got her report card last week," Paula began excitedly. "She got three As and two Bs. The only problem was that she failed gym."

"Failed gym?" I said incredulously. "You look fit enough. What happened?"

"Oh, the dike who teaches it has it in for me," Diana replied casually.

"How come?" I asked.

"I walk around naked in the locker room. You're not supposed to, but I don't see anything wrong with it. She gives me a zero every time she sees me, and believe me, she's looking." Diana laughed.

Everyone looked embarrassed. I was, too. The image of Diana parading through the locker room was a bit disconcerting.

"You're just like my parents," Diana continued, giving me time to recover. "I get all As and Bs, and you're all over my case about gym."

There was no malice in her voice. She was back to the flirty manner of our early meetings.

"Guilty as charged," I admitted with a laugh. "How are things going otherwise?"

"I imagine you mean my drinking," Charles said heartily. "Everything's going fine. I feel much better, and I think we're getting along much better."

"It does make a difference," Paula said. "It's as though he's part of the family again. We talk more, and things are more relaxed. I wish he'd spend less time in front of the T.V., though."

For the first time, I asked Martha about her school, her life, her boyfriend. She seemed friendly and available. In some ways she was more appealing than Diana. She was more womanly and had a handsome face and a strong body.

Toward the end of the session, I asked Tina about school. She was reserved and reluctant but warmed up as she went along. It became clear that although her schoolwork was satisfactory, she had few friends or interests. After school she usually amused herself. She watched a lot of T.V.

When Diana perceived my concern, she sprang to Tina's defense. "Shrinks always have to find a problem. They can't stand it when things are going well. Don't worry, Tina kid, you're the healthiest one of us."

And so I was effectively cut off from my pursuit of young Tina.

The next session went pretty much the same. We spent most of the time talking about Paula's family. It was a grim tale of drunkenness, fights, beatings, arrests. Paula's sister became a drug addict and a prostitute; her brother was thrown out of the police force for drunkenness. Paula and a brother who became a priest were the sole survivors. Her mother had had a nervous and physical breakdown shortly after her father's death and had been in a nursing home ever since. The rest of the family had heard all of this before and seemed less than fascinated. At the end of the session, Charles announced that he was planning to be out of town on business the following week. Could the rest of the family come without him? I saw no sense of urgency so I agreed to skip a week.

Charles canceled the next session by phone. Things were going very well, he said. Diana seemed happier and was doing well in school, but both Paula and Martha had the flu. He said that he missed the sessions and hoped they could make it the following week.

When the Cristie family actually arrived for their next appointment, they greeted me like a long-lost relative. Even Tina smiled. We spent the first part of the session processing a tedious argument between Diana and her mother over whether she should vacuum the living room. Martha jumped in a few times with evaluations of Diana's character, drawing the predictable reaction from Diana each time. Charles resumed his forearms-on-knees pose, and Tina's body looked without animating force. It was like old times.

I wondered how to check up on Charles's drinking without

having it appear that I was checking up on Charles's drinking. As I attempted to bring the vacuuming controversy to a satisfactory conclusion, I began to notice that Paula just would not let go of it, even though there seemed to be no more content on which to disagree. She seemed to be drawing on a vast storehouse of anger. Finally I asked her if she could define exactly what she wanted from Diana. From the position of helpless victim, Paula began another exposition of Diana's attitude; then she gave me an inquisitive look, broke off, and then said that she was angry at Charles as well. When I asked why, she said that she thought he was drinking again.

"I knew it!" Charles said with a rueful smile.

"Well, you're back to hiding in the den, and I thought you were drunk the night before last," said Paula somewhat defensively.

"Why did you think he was drunk?" I asked.

"He had that blank look on his face, and he was walking funny."

Charles laughed, but not with authenticity. "That's funny. The night before last I didn't drink at all after dinner. I didn't even watch T.V. I had a report to prepare, and I worked on it in the den."

Paula looked angry and chagrined.

Charles went on, "I stay in the den because when I come out everyone ignores me anyway. I'm a stranger in my own house." Nobody disagreed.

"So you have been able to keep to the regimen you outlined the last time we got together?" I asked.

"Yeah, pretty much."

"Pretty much?"

"Yeah, I may have gone over a couple of times in the last three weeks, but I certainly didn't get drunk. I like drinking less than I did. It was just a habit I'd fallen into."

"Does it bother you that you weren't able to stick to your plan?" I asked.

"No, I just decided to cut down. You were the one who wanted me to set a limit. I'm only concerned about not letting it get out of hand. It doesn't matter what I do, anyway. Paula won't believe me no matter what."

"How do you want them to treat you?" I asked.

"I don't know, but they just ignore me."

"Maybe they're not used to your being around. Give them a chance."

"That's a good idea. I'll try," Charles agreed.

The talk then turned to how much better Diana was; no school or drug incidents, and a generally better attitude. Martha then volunteered that she would have night classes the following semester so she could work at her nursing placement during the day. I looked at the calendar and saw that there were only a couple of weeks before vacations started, followed by the new semester.

Charles said that because things were going so well, perhaps it might be a good idea to stop therapy then. I asked what other people thought and received no reply. We would see what happened, I said, and the session ended.

The next two sessions were no more eventful than the one just reported. Charles was drinking moderately, and Diana was causing no trouble. No new issues were introduced. Charles said he felt "more welcome" in the family, and Paula stopped complaining about his isolation. I agreed to terminate treatment at vacation week. Paula presented me with a cake inscribed, "Thanks from the Cristies," and we all had a piece at the end of the session. I took the remaining cake home, where it dried to the consistency of pumice before I accepted the fact that I wasn't going to eat it.

My three-year-old son reads a magazine in which they have a game challenging him to find things wrong in a picture. It might be enlightening to think of the case just described as that sort of puzzle. In this section I will offer my observations. I do not flatter myself that I will find all the mistakes I made. Nor do I expect readers to agree with all my notions and conclusions—or even most of them. But if this material encourages readers to think about and take a position on the issues raised, I will feel the exercise has been a success. The following is a partial list of the clinical sins I committed in the Cristie case. My apologies to the Cristies. They deserved better, but it was the best I could do at the time.

1. The Truth Shall Make You Free (never lie to a client). This would seem self-evident. For most therapists, honesty is high on the list of values, and yet lying may be the most commonly committed therapeutic sin. The reason for this is that many (probably most) therapists of all disciplines are trained to expect themselves to be slightly more than human. Consider for a moment the Rogerian notion of "unconditional positive regard." Who among us has experienced unconditional positive regard for anyone, even our own children? A therapist expecting himself or herself to maintain this stance with a client is going to have many reactions that bring up the question of lying. Lies, of course, do not have to be stated verbally in order to be destructive; an implied lie can as effectively paralyze the therapist as a boldly stated falsehood.

Lying is so destructive in therapy because a lie in the context of a personal relationship renders the liar powerless in that relationship. When I lie to you in a relationship, by implication I am admitting that the person I really am is not O.K. in this relationship, and that I must pretend to be someone else to relate to you. This does not enhance my effectiveness in dealing with you. I do not have to be aware of the above facts or even to be aware of the fact that I am lying for my behavior to successfully undercut me. Let me offer an example. When I teach, I often ask my students if any of them has had experience with court referrals. When someone raises a hand, I ask the unlucky victim if he or she is willing to participate in a brief role play. Because the person has already volunteered by implication, the answer is always yes. I swagger over to that person until I am very close (I am six foot-four inches), and then I say, "My probation officer told me to talk to you. What are you supposed to talk about?" With a scowl, I move still closer, until the other person would have to be remarkably free of paranoia not to perceive an implied physical threat. My victim usually counters with, "Won't you sit down?" I reply, "I'd rather stand."

I ask the rest of the group how my victim is doing, solicit their theories as to why he is so helpless, and ask for suggestions about how the situation might be improved.

There is usually agreement that the victim is not doing very well but some confusion as to what might be done about it. Some say that the victim is sitting and I am standing and that is the problem—the victim should stand up. The drawbacks of this suggestion soon become apparent. Standing up carries an unmistakable implication of physical confrontation—certainly a no-win situation for a counselor. Even if the situation is reversed, and the counselor can face down a smaller client, the counselor loses, because he is clearly implying that the rules of the street apply in his office as well and that size and violence prevail. This is a message that counselors of delinquents might hesitate to communicate.

The counselor in this situation is rendered helpless by the fact that he is lying to his client. By sitting and calmly talking to the client he is implying, "I am not afraid or intimidated," and that implied statement is patently false. This lie allows the client to reap the benefits of intimidation without having to accept responsibility for intimidating; after all, the counselor is implying that he is not intimidated.

The move I recommend is for the counselor to say, "I wish you would sit down. When you stand over me like that, I feel very frightened and uncomfortable. Could you please sit down over there?" If the delinquent continues to loom, he must do it knowing that he is frightening the counselor. The counselor can now deal with him as he would with any assaultive client: Get help. Set limits. In nearly all cases, however, the client will sit down and explain that he has no wish to scare the counselor. The truth has set the counselor free.

When Diana Cristie walked into my office, I was distracted by her scanty attire, but I never communicated this to Diana. I interviewed her as if she were wearing the habit of a particularly conservative order of nuns. I was implying, "I am almost twice your age and a professional counselor; therefore the sight of all this skin has no effect on the way I treat you." Had I said, "I really appreciate your showing me your pretty skin, but I find it distracts me from what you're saying. You deserve my undivided attention, so could you please wear more clothes next time you come?" She would not have been in the position of being seductive without taking responsibility. We could have proceeded from a position of mutual respect and frankness. Had she needed a counselor who felt no response to her provocation, she would obviously have needed someone else. In the actual case my implied lie made me much less effective than I might have been.

2. Never attempt to get an adolescent to like you and think you are cool. The rationale for this rule is quite simple. Even the most mature, achievement-oriented and successful adolescents are convinced that, deep down, there is something wrong with them. The successful ones know that there is something wrong with them but they are successfully hiding it. Young people in trouble are sure that there is something wrong with them and that everybody knows it. If a counselor says, "I like you and respect you and want to be your friend," they find themselves in a real bind. They would like to believe the statement, but it radically clashes with their experience of reality. In order to believe it, adolescents would have to abandon their sense of the world as an understandable, predictable place (possibly our most profound psychological need). This price is too high, which leaves three interpretations of the counselor's statement. (a) The counselor is stupid; (b) The counselor knows but is lying for some reason; and (c) The counselor is both stupid and lying. This does not give the relationship the best chance to develop fruitfully. With adolescents it is better to start a relationship with a noncommittal stance and give them a chance to learn how to please you, rather than trying to please them by showing how you are like them. If they don't like themselves, and you are like them, how are they going to like you?

It was a mistake for me to tell war stories and adopt a countercultural stance with Diana. In general I believe that it is a bad idea for counselors working with adolescents to volunteer any information about their own use of drugs—past or present. It can't help, and it stands a good chance of hurting.

Suppose a counselor is asked, "Do you ever smoke dope?" A yes answer means that the counselor is using an illegal drug and has just made the client an accessory after the fact. Credibility with the client is weakened. Lame rationalizations, such as "I am mature enough to use drugs in a responsible way, and you're not," weaken credibility further. If the answer is no, the adolescent can use that as a way of distancing the relationship either by not believing the counselor or by deciding that the counselor doesn't understand the experience of adolescents. If an adolescent asks me if I smoke dope, I explain my options as above and say that I would be a damn fool to answer the questions and he or she doesn't need a damn fool as a counselor.

3. Never set a limit you cannot comfortably enforce. In my opinion this is the key rule in any work with adolescents. (It is also well known that many alcoholics can extend their adolescence into their forties, fifties, or even beyond. There is some speculation that adolescence can be preserved indefinitely in high concentrations of alcohol.)

Adolescence is a time of change, confusion, and chaos. The internal structures and rules break down and change rapidly. As a result adolescents have a profound need for something outside themselves to structure their experience. In fact adolescent societies are extremely structured as to hierarchy and acceptable behavior. Those societies that are well insulated from adult influence, such as street gangs, have a structure that is rigid and totalitarian. It can safely be said that when an adolescent is "acting out," whatever structures are responsible for setting limits on the adolescent's behavior are not functioning correctly. Effective treatment for these adolescents would therefore consist of intervening to enable these structures to set limits effectively.

Helping adolescents is so difficult because the institutions responsible for limit setting—schools, courts, families—pretend to set limits but do not. The court system, for example, will place a child on probation, setting up stringent sanctions for violating conditions of probation. But when the child tests the limit—and he or she always will—nothing happens. The child quickly learns that grownups aren't serious about limit setting. They don't mean what they say.

The counselor with an adolescent in his office should first ask himself, "Where is my leverage?" (Why is that young person sitting there, and what would happen if he wasn't.) It is useful to have plenty of leverage, i.e., a felony charge in continuance or a suspended sentence, but if you do not, *don't pretend that you do.* Admit that you have no way to enforce limits and do not try to set any.

When I told Diana that she couldn't use drugs if she wanted me to work with her, I was bluffing. Adolescents will always call your bluff. When she came in stoned, I was caught between two unattractive alternatives—(a) Back down from the limit, continue seeing her, and lose credibility; (b) Enforce the limit and lose her, effectively forcing someone out of drug treatment because she has a drug problem. In the actual case I found a third alternative, but even so, I lost face. The alternative I ran to—family therapy—was made less viable because I had violated yet another rule. This rule applies to family therapists:

4. Do not enter into alliance with an adolescent against reasonable parental authority. This is a bind that stymies many therapists who work in settings which are not primarily oriented around family work. An adolescent will be referred because he or she is experiencing some difficulty or symptom. A therapist will begin seeing the adolescent, form a relationship, gather data, and then realize that the family needs to be

seen. The therapist will invite the family and then discover that there is information which the adolescent does not want the family to have but has shared with the therapist in good faith, expecting confidentiality to be respected. The therapist has the option of: (a) exposing the information, thereby betraying the implicit contract with the adolescent and showing himself to be untrustworthy in front of the entire family, or (b) keeping the information secret, thereby entering into a conspiracy with the adolescent against the parents and sabotaging the very hierarchy the therapist is trying to empower. A possible option (c), attempting to renegotiate your contract with the adolescent so that either you or the adolescent will reveal the information, might be all right if the adolescent is willing, but will certainly make your helplessness clear to the adolescent. If the adolescent is not willing to cooperate, there are few attractive options left ("few" being a euphemism for "none"). If a therapist has this kind of relationship with an adolescent, it should be standard practice to refer the family to another therapist for treatment and to discontinue the individual work as soon as possible. There may be factors which suggest that individual work should continue, but these factors should be regarded with extreme suspicion, because the cost of maintaining individual treatment is considerable. Individual treatment implies that the problem exists in the adolescent, not in the family.

The individual therapist can provide a counterauthority which can undermine the authority of the parents but not effectively replace it. If the therapists keep the two therapies separate and do not coordinate and share information, then the adolescent's therapist must get all data from the adolescent's point of view and will find it hard not to support the adolescent, at least tacitly, in parent-child conflicts. If the information is shared and the treatments coordinated, then the family therapist will find himself in the same bind as if he, too, were seeing the adolescent separately.

For these reasons and many others, I feel that the treatment of choice for troubled adolescents is a family-treatment contract—whether or not the family is alcoholic—and that any individual work is done with the clear understanding that the family is the unit of treatment and confidentiality must be negotiated in that context.

Often when the parents think the adolescent is safely in treatment, it is difficult to motivate them to come in. In the Cristie case, Diana and I were keeping her sexual activities secret from her parents. While it may be appropriate for Diana to keep her sex life from her parents, it is highly inappropriate for me to join her. By doing so I am tacitly approving of behavior which the parents condemn. I am therefore a more understanding and permissive parent to Diana than are Charles and Paula. We can also recall the discrepancies between Diana's story of how she came to me and the story the parents told. A close examination of this would betray Diana; to avoid it was to conspire with her.

5. Do not undermine the competence or authority of the parents in a family. Arguing with parents, telling them what to do with their children in front of the children, or taking over for them in a session all imply that the parents are incompetent and that you know how they should function better than they.

My "virtuoso" performances with Diana, wherein I moved her from a frightening, out-of-control infant to an available, reasonable child were actually destructive to Diana and her parents. The implication was that Diana was reasonable if only one knew how to handle her. This was nonsense, but the parents experienced me effortlessly doing something they couldn't do. It also gave Diana the message that the way to get close to me was to stomp on her parents. Instructing her parents how to handle her reinforces these messages and brands Diana's messing up as their failure. Even if this were true, it makes them feel less powerful, less in control.

5

Second Chance:
A Better Therapy

It's now clear that the Cristies were in as much trouble when I finished with them as when I began. In addition to my other mistakes, I made the most fundamental mistake one can make with an alcoholic family: I didn't deal with the drinking. The Cristies were not atypical in the fact that I got two chances. Therapy lays many traps for those who would practice it, but it tends to give us a chance to correct our mistakes. I often think that short of lying to or sexually exploiting a client, one can't make an irretrievable mistake as a therapist, so long as one accepts responsibility for one's mistakes. Diana came close to disproving this, however, when she took a massive overdose that nearly killed her. She had been in the hospital for a week when Paula called me.

My guilt might have created the hint of blame I heard in Paula's voice as she gave me the news and asked for an appointment. I asked her how Charles was taking it, and she said he was taking it very hard. Again I thought I heard blame in Paula's voice, this time apparently directed at Charles.

When I asked what the precipitating incident seemed to be, Paula said that Martha had left the house to move in with her boyfriend, Sal. Diana had bought a bottle of champagne as a housewarming gift, but Martha had refused it. They had fought, and Diana had thrown the bottle against the wall, where it exploded, injuring Martha, Sal, and Diana herself. Sal needed stitches for a cut on his cheek, and Martha's forehead was cut only inches from her eye. Diana had a slight cut on her neck. Harsh words were spoken, and Diana ran from the apartment and burst in on Paula and Charles as they were having dinner.

Charles had asked her what was wrong, and Diana let loose with a blast of obscenities aimed at Martha initially but then including Paula and Charles. Charles, who had had some high-balls before dinner, flew into a rage and struck Diana. Diana fell, then got to her feet and ran from the house. Paula and Charles then had a bad fight during which Charles threatened to hit Paula but did not. Charles went into the den and got drunk.

When Paula woke at about seven A.M. not having slept well, she checked Diana's room, and Diana was on her bed fully dressed. Her breathing sounded peculiar. There were two white envelopes on the bed and half a glass of orange juice on the bed table. Paula saw two red capsules in one of the envelopes, tried to wake Diana, and then called the police.

At the hospital it was discovered that Diana had taken almost twice as many capsules as she would have needed to kill herself (fortunately, not all of them had dissolved). The doctors were fearful of brain damage but apparently were able to administer enough oxygen to pull Diana out of coma with no lasting effects.

Diana had seemed extremely subdued and depressed in the hospital, but the doctors said that that was normal in cases like this. She refused to talk to the psychiatrists at the hospital and had asked for me. When I heard this, I felt a wave of guilt so strong it almost took my breath away. The hospital, although reluctant, had finally given Paula permission to call me.

After drinking a Coke slowly to dissipate the shock, I decided to call Diana and tell her I was coming to the hospital. From the patient information operator I found that she had a private phone. Diana answered on the first ring with a cheery hello, and seemed overjoyed to hear from me. She sounded relaxed and animated and urged me to come right over. I was ready for anything but her casual charm and humor. On the drive to the hospital I was able to refocus myself. I knew that what I had done before had been tragically ineffective, and I resolved to help the Cristies this time around.

Since my last meeting with the Cristies, I had seen several families of similar construction with some success. Through enrollment in a family-therapy training program, I was reading Jay Haley and Salvador Minuchin and thinking about families in a new way. One of the families I had seen successfully had presented a boy as the indexed patient rather than a nubile seductive girl, and not surprisingly, I had been infinitely more effective. I was determined to go about things differently this time.

Diana was in a private room sitting in a chair by the bed reading a fan magazine. When she lowered the magazine to give me a big hello, I could see that she was wearing jeans and a shirt unbuttoned below her sternum. As I sat on the bed to talk, Diana told me that most of the nurses were assholes, but one of the doctors was a great guy and reminded her of me.

When she stopped talking, I told her that I hadn't heard what she was saying because I was too busy wondering if she was going to lean over so I could see the rest of her breast. A blush spread up her face, and then she recovered and smiled.

"What are you, a dirty old man?" she asked with a half-smile.

"Maybe, all I know is that it's hard to talk to someone whose tits are hanging out."

She looked hurt and angry, scarcely aware of her hand as it buttoned up her shirt. When she finished, her hand stayed at her throat. She seemed to be in a trance.

"After what you did, it's clear to me that you need someone to help you, not someone to stare at your chest," I said. "Why did you take the pills?"

"I don't know. I was pissed off, I guess."

"How long are you going to stay in the hospital?"

"I think I get out tomorrow. They were going to send me up to the nut ward for observation, but I convinced them I was O.K."

"You're not O.K."

"What do you mean?"

"You're the same kid in the same family as when you took the pills. You could do it again in a minute."

She started to color again, this time with anger. "I won't do it again, don't give me that bullshit."

"How do I know that? I wouldn't have thought you would do it the first time. You're not safe to walk around loose."

"You mean you want them to put me on the nut ward?" she asked.

"I don't know. I've got to talk to your parents and see what they have to say. Somebody is going to have to keep an eye on you."

"I can't believe this," she yelled. "I almost die, and he's in here busting my chops. Don't you give a shit about me?"

"You know I do. I care about you too much to take a chance that you'll succeed in killing yourself next time."

"It's my life, I can do anything I want," she claimed.

"That's true enough, but the people who care about you have to protect themselves—and that means protecting you!"

"Nobody's going to put me on a nut ward," Diana yelled, starting to regain her balance. "I'll kill myself first."

"You already gave that a shot," I said. "If I were you, I would give these suicide threats a rest for a while. If someone hears you, you may be upstairs in the psych unit for supper. Keep smiling, I'll be in touch."

Her "fuck you" caressed my ears as I left the room. I realized that I had failed to be nice, but it was hard to rebuke myself too harshly. The conversation I had just had with Diana Cristie was long overdue. There was a pay phone near the elevator. I called the Cristie home. Paula answered. I told her that I had just had a discussion with her daughter in which views were expressed forcefully and frankly and that I wanted to convene a family meeting before Diana was discharged from the hospital.

Paula said that she wasn't sure that Martha would come— Martha was still furious at Diana and fed up with the family meetings anyway. I told Paula that while I very much wanted Martha to attend, it was essential to have a meeting before Diana's discharge even if only Paula, Charles, and Diana attended. I also asked for a letter authorizing the psychiatrist who was following Diana to speak with me.

Paula said that she would set up a time with me and clear it with Charles. She would try to get Martha to come and asked if she should bring Tina if Martha refused. I said that Tina should come in any case. Paula promised that she would send a letter to the hospital authorizing them to release information to me.

All things considered, the hospital was quite cooperative. They were not eager to take out a paper on Diana and commit her; she had succeeded in convincing them that she was sufficiently manipulative so that an inpatient evaluation was unlikely to be productive. She had no thought disorder and explained her overdose as a reactive impulse (their words) which would never happen again. They agreed that I could meet the family in the hospital once. The psychiatrist who had supervised me on the Cristie case before was on the staff of the hospital, and he facilitated matters. The meeting took place the evening after I had visited Diana, in the modern cheery dayroom on Diana's floor. Anything that removed us from the scene of previous failure was welcome. As I had hoped, Martha was present, looking sullen perhaps, but present nevertheless. Tina's body was there, too, neatly dressed and groomed, although her face wore its familiar catatonic patina.

Paula sat on the edge of her chair looking tense and angry, and Charles was slumped forearms on knees. Diana chatted amiably with Paula, seemingly oblivious to Paula's taut disapproving glances. I consciously steeled myself for what had every diagnostic indicator of a long and difficult evening.

"I'm glad you could all come," I began, "because this is a

very serious situation, and everyone is going to have to work hard to improve it." No response.

"Charles," I said, turning my chair to face him. "What do you think we ought to do?"

"I don't know," he mumbled. "I've never known what to do with Diana since she was a little kid."

"Well, I don't think anyone else has done any better than you have, and she's seen lots of folks who are supposed to be experts."

"You know how to relate to her," said Charles, looking up with sad eyes. "She's always listened to you and respected you. We don't know what we would do without you." Paula nodded vigorously. It was nice to see the parents in agreement, even if they were agreeing that I should do their job for them.

"Oh, yeah, I did a great job. That's why we're all here in the hospital. No, it's you folks who are going to fix this situation, not me."

"What do you mean?" Paula asked.

"Just that this family has all the resources it needs to help Diana get squared away. How many people do you supervise at work, Charles?"

"At work? About fifty-two, why?" said Charles, surprised at the sudden shift in subject.

"How many do you directly supervise?"

"Nine supervisors report directly to me," he said.

"What does this have to do with anything?" Diana asked in a whiny voice.

"Bear with me," I said, not looking at her. "Do you do a good job supervising these people?" I asked.

"My company thinks so," Charles said, sounding a trifle hostile.

"What makes them think so?" I pushed.

"The performance of my division improved nearly thirty percent since I took over."

"How much of that do you figure is due to your leadership?" I asked.

"Quite a bit, actually. Only two of my supervisors came

since I took over, and I inherited most of the line staff, too. It took me a while to get things working right, and it was rough, especially in the beginning.''

''But everyone was cooperative?''

''For the most part. Of course, there were a few guys who didn't get the picture right away, but most of them came around.''

''How did you get them to come around?''

''I just made it clear what I expected of them and tried to give them the overall picture. I also made it clear what would happen if they couldn't fit into the picture. I only had to transfer one supervisor and two staff; the rest came around even better than I hoped.'' Charles was now on the edge of his seat, his eyes clear and focused. I had never seen him look like this. I wondered if his family had. Charles had been hypnotized— he was hallucinating that he was at work and feeling the energy and confidence he felt in that environment. I touched his shoulder to anchor those feelings. I was going to need them, but now it was time to pull the rug out from under him.

''You know, I'm struck by the contrast between how you function at work and how you function in this family. This family needs someone with your energy and leadership skills at least as much as Casualty Insurance does. How do you account for the fact that they're not getting it?''

Charles looked stunned. His eyes began to lose their clarity; he began to slump.

''I don't know,'' he said, almost by reflex.

''Maybe it's because he doesn't drink at work,'' Paula said. ''If he had a few highballs the minute he walked in the office, he wouldn't do anything there either!''

I touched Charles's shoulder, hoping to pull some of his good energy back. (Pavlov showed that if a stimulus occurred at the same time as a strong feeling, the nervous system would link the stimulus to the feeling so that an exposure to the stimulus would access the feeling. Bandler and Grinder systematize this in the *Structure of Magic,* Vol. II, but advertisers have been utilizing it for years.)

"Well, if they treated me the way you do, I'd probably drink there, too!" Charles exploded.

"So now it's my fault you drink?" Paula countered.

"Well, you *are* always putting him down, Ma," Martha put in. Another country heard from.

"I think this is between your parents, Martha," I said, touching Charles's knee again and looking expectantly at him.

This was a good example of the subtle tactics a family can use to counter a move to change them. I was trying to start an exchange between a strong, competent Charles and his wife. Martha's defense of Charles (1) deflected the exchange from Charles and Paula to Martha and Paula; (2) carried the implication that Charles could not take care of himself and needed her to represent him; (3) weakened the boundary between parents and children, so that children could move in and undercut the hierarchy in the family.

"She's always putting her two cents in," Diana interjected. They were ganging up on me, although the two girls fully believed they were fighting with each other. I was perceiving them as a precision team of saboteurs hitting me high and low.

"You know," I said, addressing Diana and Martha, "you two are doing a great job of keeping your parents from fighting. I guess you know better than I do when it's getting heavy enough to be dangerous. If you don't mind, I would like to give both of you the job of interrupting if they begin to scare you. Have things already gotten too far, or are you willing to let them continue?" They looked stunned and sullen, but both nodded.

"Charles, you said that the people at Casualty treat you differently from the way Paula does. What do you mean?"

Charles was much less vibrant than before the girls intervened, but he tried to gather himself. "At work they show me confidence and respect. The minute I get home, I'm treated like an idiot."

"What do you think you would do if they treated you that way at work?" I said, leaning to touch his knee again and maintain eye contact.

"I would set them straight soon enough," he said.

"Set them straight," I said.

"I want you all to start treating me with a little respect. I work hard to provide a good home, and I think that should be acknowledged," Charles said, but he didn't believe a word of it. He was not alone.

"You want us to salute you when you pass out in your chair and pee your pants?" Diana asked.

"You're the one to talk, you little junkie," Martha chimed in.

"Fuck you." Where had I heard that before?

"I guess it's getting too hot again, eh, kids?" (I used the word *kids* purposely and stressed it, hoping to communicate at an unconscious level that there were two groups here: kids and parents.)

"You know," I went on, "I'm not sure whether your parents have hired you as their attorneys or whether you just volunteered. But I keep noticing that whenever your *parents* get into a discussion, you *kids* take it over for them. Martha, you seem to agree with me that your father is entitled to more respect, and Diana, you seem to disagree. Seeing as you don't seem to want your parents to discuss this, I wonder if you would be willing to discuss it for them. Martha, could you explain to Diana why she and the family as a whole should show your father more respect, and try to talk about your father, not about Diana. Diana, if she starts talking about you, could you remind her by saying, 'Fuck you!' "

"I don't need Martha to argue my case for me," Charles said, his energy returning. "I'm the father in this family, and it's not such a bad family. Everyone has enough to eat, nice clothes, and a good home. If Diana doesn't appreciate it, she can live somewhere else and see how she likes it!"

"Material things aren't everything, Charles," said Paula, finally entering the fray. "These children haven't had a father from the day they were born. They don't think they are important to you, and neither do I."

"Everybody seems to think I'm an alcoholic and a bum,"

Charles said, raising his voice, but without the ring of confidence. "It's not true, and I'll prove it by stopping right now."

"Wait a minute," I said. "I don't want you to stop drinking for them or to prove anything to them. I sense that you are comfortable with your drinking and want to continue. Don't let them think they can control your drinking. Only *you can stop your drinking.* It's not up to them. *It's your job,* and *you'll do it* if you *decide to take the job.*

"The rest of this is too confusing. I don't want anything to change too fast. That's what happened last time. Let's just hold our horses and discuss this next week. You can all use that time to consider what *jobs* you want to *do in this family.* Until then there is plenty to think about."

I stood up. Charles, Paula, Diana, and Martha stood up, too. Tina continued to sit, but her catatonic glaze was gone. She was looking at me with a calm, level gaze—a disconcerting look from an eleven-year-old. I wondered if she was on to me.

Afterward I had a chance to review the session in my mind. It was striking how different this session felt from all of the others with this family. Part of the difference could be accounted for by the time gap and the far more dramatic presenting problem. The overdose certainly was tangible evidence of the failure of the previous treatment, but it also served to impress everyone with the gravity of the problem, which in turn provided me with more leverage with the family.

But time and even the overdose were not, to my mind, sufficient to explain the difference in the way I felt. The family seemed much the same, even after two years, and while the overdose certainly got the family's attention, they had apparently been very concerned the first time around.

No, to my mind the session felt different because I had some sense of what was wrong with the Cristie family and what I planned to do about it. It is hard to overstress the importance of developing a clear hypothesis and game plan before seeing a family. Whether the hypothesis is accurate or the plan viable is much less important than the simple existence of hypothesis and plan. Forming and stating a hypothesis forces the therapist to take responsibility for a theory as to what is going on. Moreover, it provides a filter and filing system which will help process the enormous volume of data that a family can generate in just a few minutes. Once a hypothesis is formed and stated, data will naturally divide itself into three categories: data which tends to confirm the hypothesis, data which tends to deny it, and data which is ambiguous. The next hypothesis must somehow make peace with the data which did not fit the previous hypothesis, and there must also be a plan to pin down ambiguous data.

For example, in the Cristie family my hypothesis was that Diana's problems were due to the fact that her parents were unable to form a coalition to regulate her behavior. My understanding of the factors which prevented this coalition focused around Charles's drinking. I had no idea whether Charles drank because he was peripheral and excluded, or whether he was peripheral and excluded because he drank, but this chicken-and-egg question was of academic interest only. The main question was how to get him to abridge his role of passive drunk and start learning the husband and father business.

Any plan directed toward this end must necessarily consider that any change in Charles's functioning would cause discomfort and therefore resistance from every member of the family and from the system as a whole. One positive aspect of my previous failure with the Cristies was that I had had a considerable period in which to watch them.

One very basic fact of human systems in general and families in particular is that they develop sequences of behavior which repeat. The Cristie family had several such sequences which I could identify. When a therapist discovers a sequence which stabilizes a dysfunctional structure in the family, the therapist must interfere with that sequence. It is not to be assumed that the family will change if the sequence is stopped, it is simply that change is much less likely to occur if that sequence is allowed to continue.

In the case of the Cristies, I was trying to change Charles's position in the family from incompetent and marginal to competent and central. The dance of Paula attack Charles / Diana attack Charles / Martha attack Diana / Diana attack Martha had occurred over and over.

When I had first treated the family, I found this dance annoying but had no idea what it did for the family. In the context of putting pressure on the parents to act like parents, the function on this sequence became clear. Equally clear was the fact that it had to be stopped. Once I knew what I was trying to do, I could categorize data I received by observing the family behave: behavior which made it easier to achieve my goal, behavior which made it harder, and behavior which fit neither category. This last category of data told me what was missing from my hypothesis.

Before the next session I would clarify my own goals: to get Charles into his powerful persona and then get him to join with Paula to decide how the family should be run and how the children, particularly Diana, should behave. Once this was decided, they would then have to invent a realistic plan as to how this must be enforced.

It would also be useful for me to identify the most obvious obstacles to achieving these goals:

1. Charles's drinking, which allowed himself and other family members not to consider him a positive resource;

2. a family interactive pattern which excluded Charles and defined him as useless and inappropriate;

3. the repetitive pattern of the two above factors reenforcing each other.

The Cristies were about seven minutes late for the session—just long enough for me to start thinking of reasons why they might not come. The moment they arrived, it was obvious that if I had pushed them off balance the week before, they had taken advantage of the opportunity to regain their equilibrium. Diana entered first, with a medium-sullen look; then came

Paula, looking tense and angry; then Martha, looking impatient and bored; then Tina, doing her android imitation; and finally—after a ten-second gap—Charles himself. The slump of his shoulders indicated that my work was cut out for me. Nor was I encouraged by the fact that he had shed his usual immaculate dress for an outfit that suggested he had spent the day cleaning the cellar.

Charles avoided my eye and quickly assumed the head-down-forearms-on-knees pose, which I interpreted to mean that he wasn't at his best.

Paula, on the other hand, had no trouble meeting my eye. She perched at the edge of her customary chair and said, "Sorry we're late. We had trouble getting out of the house."

"Trouble getting out of the house?" I asked.

"Yes. Charles took the day off to relax, and he relaxed so much that we could barely wake him for the session."

"He was shitfaced," was Diana's contribution.

"Why do you always have to open your garbage mouth?" Martha said.

"Fuck you!"

"Don't you start," Paula warned.

"Don't get on my case. I'm not the one who's shitfaced," Diana retorted.

"You think we should give you a prize every time you're not zapped out on drugs?" Martha said.

"Fuck you in the ear, Miss Perfect!"

"I don't have to take that from you, you little snot!"

"Girls, girls!" Paula said.

"Don't call me a . . ." Diana began.

"Didn't you hear your mother?" I said, bringing my voice up from the diaphragm. Diana stopped and glared at me.

"It's hard to see how this is going to get us anywhere," I said in my sternest voice.

"Were you drinking, Charles?" I asked. I couldn't see how this could be avoided. Charles mumbled something unintelligible; his eyes were fixed on a stain on the rug.

I could feel a wave of anger as I observed this piteous sight. Careful, I told myself, he's going to get you in a second.

Moments like these are important choice points for therapists working with alcoholic families. The trap yawns. It would be so easy to join the family in abusing Charles. I could feel myself slipping into trance. At a hypnosis workshop Dr. Bennett Braun had said, "If you are not hypnotizing them, they are hypnotizing you." I had a feeling this is what he meant.

I was well set up. I had invested a lot of energy the previous week trying to get Charles to look very different from this. I had trotted out a lot of advanced technique; I had finished the session with a sense of satisfaction. And now look.

Moments like these point up the importance of accepting responsibility for your results. The fact that I consciously accept responsibility for my goals and results empowers me to make a choice about what to do when my employers fall short of my wishes for them. It gives me a chance to avoid the rescue triangle, because I *know* I am ego-involved in their behavior.

I can choose not to blame Charles for my behavior and abuse him in subtle or not-so-subtle ways. One trait shared by almost all alcoholics is an uncanny ability to irritate people, particularly people who are trying to help them. You cannot help people change if you are induced to treat them the way everyone else does.

"Charles," I said in a hearty tone. "I have to hand it to you. You are an artist. Your performance is nearly perfect. I would have been fooled if it weren't for last week."

I watched Charles to see if he would bite. No luck. He remained fascinated by the Australia-shaped stain in the rug.

"Look at you—the repentant sinner. Eyes down, bent over, mumbling voice. I sincerely doubt if one member of this family knows enough to be grateful to you. I'm not sure you shouldn't sit like that until they understand."

That got him. "What do you mean?" he mumbled.

"Listen to that mumble. You sound so ashamed of yourself. I bet you don't even realize how you are getting this whole family off the hook. Are you still drunk?''

"No, I'm not still drunk!'' Finally Charles sat erect. "What are you talking about?''

"I'll explain in a minute, but first I have to know what happened this afternoon.''

"I had a meeting canceled, and I've been going flat out for a long time, so I decided to take the day off and relax.''

"You relaxed your way through half a bottle of scotch,'' Paula said.

"I admit I had a few highballs this afternoon, but I wasn't bothering anyone.''

"It bothered me to hear you with that snore in the middle of the afternoon. It bothered me when I could hardly wake you up this evening.''

"You should have seen the old lush lying there with his mouth wide open,'' Diana said.

I saw Martha gathering for the attack. Time to move.

"Diana,'' I said, "this is between your parents. They don't need your help.''

"Bullshit.''

"You listen carefully. If you think they need help, you tell me. I'm the therapist here, not you.''

She gave me a quizzical look, then winked at Tina. Tina didn't react. I turned back to Charles.

"I did have too much to drink this afternoon,'' he said, "but it's the first time I drank all week.''

"What?'' I said.

"It's true. Charles had been very good this week up to today,'' Paula confirmed.

"You were a good boy this week, Charles?'' I asked.

"I wasn't being a good boy,'' Charles said with irritation. "I just didn't feel like drinking.''

"And nobody in the family noticed, so you decided to tie one on today,'' I said.

"We did so notice,'' Diana burst in. "I noticed from the first day, but I was afraid to say anything.'' Tears were welling in her eyes. This was not the slick little smartass we all knew and loved.

I looked at Martha and saw only an expression of irritation, but Tina's eyes were also filling up. It was the first sign of life I had seen from her since she did the family sculpture. Paula was misting, too. Tears can be more contagious than the flu. It was amazing what a little honest emotion can do for a family. My eyes were beginning to sting. I moved closer to Charles.

"Look around," I said. "You didn't know you could make such a difference, did you?"

"Oh, Daddy," Diana cried out, "it was great when you were awake and would talk and joke. It was even different watching T.V. with you."

Tina nodded, tears patterning her cheeks.

"All of a sudden you're the loving daughter, you little liar," Martha snapped.

Charles looked at Martha with a sad look and held up his hand. Martha and Diana were quiet.

"Martha was trying to help us get back to normal," I said. "I'm not used to this family either, and it must be a lot stranger for all of you." Nobody spoke.

"Are you surprised you make such a difference here?" I asked Charles again.

"Yes," he said.

"I think you already knew. I think that's why you got drunk today."

"What do you mean?"

"When you don't drink, everyone is happy, but they're also uncomfortable. They don't know what to make of you when the vice-president comes home and stays a vice-president. If you don't drink, you put everyone in the family on the hook. Maybe you were afraid Diana would take another overdose to get things back to normal. I don't know. Anyway, you got drunk so Paula could go back to being angry, Tina could go back to her coma, Diana could go back to being a delinquent, and Martha could go back to protecting you. If you don't drink, everyone's going to have to learn a new act.''

Silence.

"So I guess you'll all go back to business as usual this week.''

"Not a chance,'' said Charles, smiling, "I'm staying on the wagon.''

"Not so fast,'' I said. "You're making it sound like the easiest thing in the world. It's very hard to stop drinking without help, and if you drink after that promise, all these folks will give up on you and everything will go back to the way it was. This is not something to be taken lightly. Do you know how hard it is to quit drinking?''

"I can do it; I'm not an alcoholic.''

"I'm not saying you are. I'm asking if you are really serious about quitting drinking.''

"Yes, I am.''

"Why are you quitting? I know you like to drink.''

"Because I realize how much difference it makes to my family.''

"So you're going to make a big sacrifice for them. What are you going to get in return?''

"I don't expect anything!'' Charles said, looking sullen.

"Look, Saint Charles, I can't believe you rose to vice-president of a major insurance company making deals like that. Drinking has been important to you. It's the way you relax and unwind; it's been your solace and comfort, right?''

"Yeah.''

"And you're telling me that you're going to give it up for these folks without asking anything in return?''

"That's right,'' defiantly.

"Do you folks believe him?''

The kids looked stunned. Paula's face hardened.

"No, I don't. He's made promises before. Lots of times.''

Charles reddened.

"See,'' I said, "no gratitude even. I bet you feel like going back to drinking right now if this is all the thanks you get.''

"Yeah, I do.''

"So you couldn't hold your resolve even for a minute in the

face of your family, and there are going to be a lot of moments like this. Your quitting drinking is as scary for them as it is for you. I think you are going to need help. I have a friend who has been in A.A. a long time. Can I ask him to call you up and take you to a meeting?''

"I don't need A.A. I'm not an alcoholic."

"That may well be. I don't know. There are people who quit drinking without A.A. There are also people who fly without a parachute. I don't know whether you can or not. If you can, there's no problem, but what if you can't? What if you drink again?'' Check.

"Then I guess I'll go to A.A."

"Is that just a guess, or is that a commitment?'' Check.

"It's a commitment."

"So if you have even one drink—a short beer on a hot day, wine at communion, a toast to the bride, anything—you promise to go to A.A. with my friend?'' Checkmate.

"Yes, I do."

"Now,'' I said, addressing the family. "You play a big part in this, too. I don't think any of you believed Charles when he said he was willing to stop drinking without expecting anything in return, so I'm afraid you will make little silent deals to be really nice to him and keep the pressure off him. You'll tiptoe around as if he was telling the truth or even if he can quit drinking."

"What do you mean,'' Paula asked.

"If he can only quit drinking if you treat him like a china doll, you'll wind up dreading the first wrong move that will start the whole dance again. Also, if you leave him out of the pain and pressure of the family, then he might as well be drinking. The best thing this family can do is to treat him like a husband and a father. Push him, don't let him retreat into his room. Diana, you are going to have to mess up to see if he and your mom are up to dealing with you. In fact you might start planning some screwup right now."

"What? You're asking me to screw up?"

"Yes, I am, and I realize that I'm taking a risk, because if you do something that hurts you, I'll be to blame. I better know what you're planning to do."

"I'm not planning to do anything."

"Then how will you know if your parents can come through for you?" No reply. "Do you two think you can set limits on Diana if she makes trouble, because she is sure to test you. She has to know that you can work together, and I'm sure she will provide you with an opportunity to learn."

Charles began to look hopeful. "Diana, look, I'll make a deal with you," he said. "I'll stay off booze if you'll stay off drugs and behave in school."

"Okay," said Diana.

"Wait a minute," I said. "Let me get this straight—Charles, if Diana uses drugs or skips school then you'll start drinking again?"

"Uh, no. I just thought . . ."

"I know it's a tempting idea because at first it seems like the same problem, but it's different. You're a parent, so you're in charge of your own behavior. Diana's a kid, so she needs her parents to be in charge until she can do a better job of taking care of herself."

"I can take care of myself!"

"Yeah, the people in the emergency room told me you almost took care of yourself for good," I said.

"You bastard, that's not fair! I'll never do that again!"

"It *is* fair. You made it really clear that you need your parents to take care of you, and I wish I could believe you won't do it again!"

I looked at my watch. We had run ten minutes over.

"Paula," I said, realigning myself with the parents, "you've been very quiet. Before we stop, I want to check in and see what you're thinking."

"Well, I hope Charles can do it this time. I've prayed for so many years."

"I get the impression you don't think he can."

"I didn't say that! It's just that he's promised before."

"I know. Well, I think he might surprise you. After all, the worst that can happen is that he'll take a drink and find out he needs A.A. You were really serious about that, weren't you, Charles?''

"Yes, I was," he said.

"Well, do Charles a favor and don't treat him with kid gloves. He's got to know he can deal with this family sober. Martha, I am wondering what's on your mind.''

"Nothing. I hope he can do it. I'm afraid Diana will screw it up.''

"There's no way Diana can make your father drink if he doesn't want to. I hope she tries. Tina, what are you thinking?''

"This was a good meeting," Tina said, rewarding me with a smile. I was surprised at how powerfully it affected me.

"See you next week," I said, trying to keep my voice clear and avoiding Diana's glare.

After they left, I sat motionless for a spell. I felt drained and blank. The only sure conclusion I had about the session was that I had talked too much. As I began to relax, I realized how tense I had become during the session. It takes a lot out of me to make a group of people I like very much as uncomfortable as I had made the Cristies. Probably my tension partially explained my loquaciousness. When people are under tension, they usually become much more active or much less active. I, of course, know which way *I* go, but I had not checked myself closely enough during the session. Talking a lot is also a way of rescuing the family. As long as I am talking, they can be passive and not interact.

On the other hand, I might also grant myself credit for making some potentially useful moves around the key issue in the Cristie family, indeed any alcoholic family: the drinking. It will be interesting to see how they respond to the session, I thought. If this session had as much impact as the one in the hospital had seemed to have, I would be satisfied—motor-mouth and all.

Some day (when I am very experienced), I will not be thrown when a family regresses. I will immediately recognize it as a sign of progress and feel optimistic and in control. I look forward to that day. However, I must admit that I was shaken when the Cristies came in as regressed as they did. They looked worse than on the first day I saw them, and they seemed angry at me. Again, I look forward to the day when I am not shaken by my clients' anger at me, although it is foolish—when I consciously and deliberately make moves to anger a client—to feel shaken when the anger comes. I keep telling clients that one cannot control one's feelings, but that shouldn't apply to therapists.

In spite of my initial reaction to the Cristies' regression, it proved to be a response to progress. I had worked very hard to push them out of equilibrium, and it is natural to expect that anything pushed out of equilibrium will swing back, like a pendulum. The previous session seemed to have a real impact. Charles had not had a drink for several days—quite a feat for a daily drinker.

Of course, there is no way of knowing what caused the changes in the Cristie family, but for whatever reason the family had been able to deal with the drinking directly tonight, and everyone had come through handsomely! Diana, particularly, had made her feelings so clear that it would be hard for Charles to ignore them.

I wondered if my dig about the family not noticing that Charles wasn't drinking had facilitated Diana's expressing her feelings so powerfully. Would things have been blander had I merely asked if people had noticed? Perhaps her outrage at my insensitivity put her in contact with her tender feelings for her father under all that hostility. Tina's and Paula's reactions were also encouraging. They seemed willing to deal with Charles on an emotional level. Only Martha, Charles's bodyguard, seemed to stay true to form. I wondered what was happening inside her. She had a lonely and thankless task.

I felt good about the way I had worked with the family around Charles's drinking. I had been careful to avoid the role of "the voice of sobriety." I would not ask Charles if he wanted to try to not drink this week; I assumed he would go back to drinking, giving him the chance to decide to quit in spite of the insensitive therapist who was selling him short.

Once he announced his intentions, I made him fight every inch of the way for his right to quit. Raising objection after objection gave the whole family a chance to anticipate what some of the problems were likely to be and to give some exercise to the part of Charles that wanted to quit drinking. As he met my objections, quitting became more and more his decision, something he fought for.

It was important to get Paula to express her doubts so that she was the voice of doubt and Charles could defy her by quitting (just as he had defied her by drinking). Predicting and prescribing the family's homeostatic reaction was also important. I always assume that when the alcoholic quits, the family will facilitate his starting up again. I wanted to undercut the family, keep them from taking over Charles's decision, taking on the responsibility to keep him sober by protecting and further infantilizing him. This is one of the more common ways families make it easy for the alcoholic to get back to drinking. Another common excuse to resume drinking lies at the other end of the spectrum—when the family fails to express gratitude and puts pressure on the alcoholic. Following Milton Erickson's technique, I chose to reframe this positively as the family testing Charles's resolve and determination so that his resentment could be expressed by refusing to drink.

The trickiest part of the whole session was to introduce the idea of A.A. without fighting the battle of "alcoholism." Charles was in no way ready to accept the label of alcoholic, and I didn't want to waste energy on selling him alcoholism that could be used to get him to stop drinking. Therefore, A.A. was framed as a tool that people use to help them stop drinking. If Charles chose to stop drinking to prove he didn't need A.A., I was quite willing to accept that. In fact, at the moment, I preferred it.

I preferred it because if Charles accepted himself as suffering from the disease of alcoholism, he would become a sick person who must put "first things first" and turn his attention to staying sober. There would be a time during which he would appropriately be discouraged from putting much energy into learning to ally with Paula in order to solve Diana's problems. He, rather than Diana, would be the "sick" one in the family. In my effort to establish a functional hierarchy in the Cristie family, I would rather have a sick kid than a sick parent. If Charles could stay sober, A.A. and the concept of alcoholism was certainly a strong fallback position, and I took care to establish it during the first glow of optimism.

My final move of the session was to reestablish Diana as the "problem" so I could keep the pressure on Charles and Paula to learn to handle her. In prescribing that Diana act out and then back down and disown acceptance of any attempt she might make to hurt herself, I set a limit without appearing to do so. Admitting my "mistake" took the power away from any dramatic demonstration of it (something she had already proved herself ready to do). Confidently predicting her acting out would give Paula and Charles a chance to get their act together if she chose to defy me by adopting saintly ways. If she obediently acted out, I could credibly reframe whatever she did as an opportunity to test Charles's resolve and demonstrate to her parents the necessity of putting their differences aside and developing a plan for managing her.

The Cristies arrived right on time for their next session. Diana and Tina entered first, joking and giggling. Paula followed close behind. She gave me a warm smile and sat in her customary chair but sat back in it rather than perching on the edge. Martha represented the conservative faction; she sat down quickly without acknowledging me. Then Charles strode in. His gait was erect, his eye was clear, his voice as he greeted me was cheerful, manly, and resonant. Uh-oh, I thought. I was half-expecting Norman Rockwell to follow them in and set up his easel. A.A. has a term which describes exquisitely what I was witnessing—"pink cloud."

"How are things going, folks?" I asked.

"Pretty good," Charles offered modestly.

"It's been a good week," said Paula. "Charles hasn't touched a drop. He's been helping me clean up after dinner and last weekend he was with Diana and Tina all day and then took us out to dinner and a movie."

"He promised to take us to a rock concert next weekend," Diana added, radiating waves of wholesomeness.

"I've never been to a rock concert before," Tina said. The android had been replaced by a lively preadolescent girl.

I had an impulse to cast the whole bunch in bronze and put them on my mantelpiece as a mute, but eloquent testament to my genius. I hated to spoil it. Ah well, art is not eternal.

"How was your week, Martha?" I asked.

"O.K.," she said, not meeting my eye.

"O.K.?" I asked. "O.K.? Everyone in here seems ready to jump out of their skins with happiness and you say O.K.? I gather you are not impressed?"

"No, I'm happy, too," she said.

"But a little suspicious, eh? Well, I'm with you." She did not show much gratitude for my support.

"As I remember, you're trained as a nurse, aren't you?" I asked.

"That's right." She answered only after it became obvious that I was not going to continue.

"As a nurse, I wonder what you would think if I had been laid up with the flu or something for weeks and then went out and played ball the minute the fever broke?"

"I'd think that you were pushing your luck," she answered, less grudgingly.

"Is that what you think is happening here?"

"I don't know."

"Let me rephrase that. Is that what you are *afraid might* be happening here?"

"I guess so." her eyes were beginning to shine. That's fine, she missed out on all the tears last week.

"You must feel very left out and lonely," I said softly. Her breathing began to spasm, and through the tears I thought I saw cold fury directed at me. She really resented losing control.

"If you were my daughter, I'd want to give you a hug, but I wouldn't know if it would be welcome or not," I said.

Charles had enough left to take the chance. Rising from the couch, he kneeled beside Martha's chair and put his arm around her shoulders. At first she hesitated, then put her head on Charles's shoulder and used the handkerchief he had magically produced.

Charles returned to the couch.

"Martha always gives and never gets," Paula said. "I could always count on her to be mature and practical even when she was a little girl, but I never knew what she was thinking. I don't think I've seen her cry in years and years."

"I sometimes worry about Martha," Charles said. "She always looks out for everyone else. I'm worried that her boyfriend will take advantage of her generous nature."

"Don't start with Sal," Martha said. "He loves me and doesn't take advantage of me."

"I don't know, Martha." This from Paula, "Sal does have a hard time holding a job and he seems to borrow money from you."

"It's my money. Besides, Sal is starting a job next week that will send him to college if it works out."

"Martha," I said, "I get the feeling you are more worried at this moment about your present family than your future one."

"Yes," she said, "I am. Dad is trying to be cheerful and be with us, and Mom means well and really appreciates it, but she's always making little criticisms and digs, and I know how sensitive he is, even though he never says anything. And I just know Diana is going to do something stupid and Dad and Mom will fight and everything will go back to the way it was."

'Fuck you, how the fuck do you know what's going to happen?" Diana demanded.

"What about you, Paula?" I asked. "Are you as sure as Diana is that Martha is wrong?"

"I don't know. I wasn't aware that I criticized Charles that much—expecially this week." Paula looked more puzzled then angry.

"Oh, you criticized him more than usual this week because he was around more this week," Martha said. "I'm afraid if you keep it up, he'll go back to the den and stay there." Martha clearly felt it her duty to protect Dad from all comers, not just Diana.

"Martha's right, Mom. You have been on Dad's case a lot," Diana said.

The drama of Diana supporting her father was not lost on the Cristies. Everyone stared at Diana as if she had metamorphosed into another species.

Reddening, Paula turned to Charles. "Have I really been that critical of you?"

"I'm not sure I noticed," Charles said uneasily.

"You do so notice," Martha said. "I can see you getting angry."

"You never say anything," Paula said to Charles.

"Well, I know how I've disappointed you over the years. I know I haven't been much of a husband or father, so I figure I deserve it."

"Well, I think it's been easy for me to blame you for everything," Paula said, her eyes beginning to fill.

"I think I have been to blame for everything," Charles said gallantly.

"Don't flatter yourself," I said. "How can you possibly be responsible for more than half of the problems you two have? The myth that Charles is mostly to blame for your problems is what keeps things so screwed up."

They looked puzzled.

"Do you know what I mean?" They both shook their heads. "It's not complicated. It's just that when you think someone is to blame for a problem you have, you are helpless to do anything about it. You have to wait for the other person to change. Charles takes the whole blame on, and if he tries to change he discovers that he can't make everything fine and gives up, so you wind up with two smart people and nobody is working on the problem. So Diana starts to test you, and Paula blames Charles, and Charles blames himself and tries to fix it himself and fails and blames Diana and gives up. Nobody's running the show.''

"What can we do about it?'' Paula said in a quiet voice.

"You've already done a lot,'' I told her. "There is no question that all of you are making a real effort to change things. The problem is that old habits die hard. There are ways of changing habits pretty quickly, but they can be difficult, even painful.''

"What kinds of ways?'' Paula asked.

"Well, you and the girls were talking about your habit of criticizing Charles. Now obviously that reinforces the myth that keeps you two stuck. The problem is that by now the behavior is so habitual and automatic that you are no more aware of doing it than you would be aware of swallowing when your throat is dry. So even if you try to stop, you can't. I could suggest a little game you two could play that might make you both aware of the process in a different way.''

"What game?'' Charles asked with interest. I was glad to see him looking more active in the process of getting Paula off his case.

"Well, it's based on the simple fact that making an unconscious act conscious will change it. For instance, if I said, 'Tina, I noticed how gracefully you walk. Could you please show us how you walk?' I would guess Tina would not walk the way she usually does.

"So the game is this. Charles will see how many times he can get Paula to criticize him each day. Charles will keep score and remember each criticism. He will probably have to take notes. Then at an appointed time, maybe after supper, you two can meet and talk about it. It might be better to do it out of the house—at a coffee shop or something.''

"So I'm supposed to try to get her to criticize me? What good will that do?'' Charles asked.

"It will change her criticism from something that happens

to you to something you *cause* to happen.''

"How do I know when he is trying to get me to criticize him and when he's not?'' Paula asked.

"You don't.''

"So any time I say something, he might just be playing with me?''

"Right.''

"What do we talk about at the meeting?'' Charles wanted to know.

"You tell Paula what criticisms she made of you and how you manipulated her to make them. Paula can tell you what was on her mind when she made them. Charles, you should pick three criticisms you feel you deserve most and ask Paula to make them again. If she doesn't do it right, you can show her how and get her to do it again. Of course, this is very strong medicine, Paula, and I certainly wouldn't blame you for not agreeing to do it.''

"No, I'll do it, if you think it will help.''

"I sure hope it will. I wouldn't want to put you through this for nothing.''

"Do we play any part in this?'' Diana asked.

"No, let's keep it between your parents.''

I used the silence that ensued to wonder how I was going to bring up the drinking.

"Anyway, you guys might even find the game is fun. Good healthy competition. I should stress having your meetings out of the house. It makes it easier to stay out of old patterns if you're not home. Go to a restaurant or a bar or even drive around in the car.''

"I'm not going to bars these days,'' Charles said firmly.

"Right, I stand corrected. How is that going?''

"Great. No problems. I must admit I feel a lot better. Lots more energy. I didn't realize how much it was affecting me.''

"What do you mean?''

"Well, drinking must have really slowed me down, because I feel so much more energetic when I don't drink.''

"So you're going to continue on the wagon?''

"Sure."

"Till when?"

"What do you mean?"

"How long are you planning not to drink?"

"I haven't thought about it."

"This might be a good time to."

"I really don't know."

"Well," I said, "I don't know either, but I get the impression that it won't be long."

"What do you mean?" Charles asked with a trace of sullenness.

"Well, I've worked with a lot of people on drinking, and it's been my experience that when a person who has been drinking as long as you have then has as easy a time stopping as you have, they usually don't last too long."

"Why not?" Charles seemed genuinely interested.

"I don't know. Maybe they get bored because it seems so easy. Maybe their defenses aren't up, so when the impulse hits them, they drink before they know what hit them. Could be a lot of things."

"Well, it won't happen to me," Charles said, not so sure now.

"I genuinely hope you're right," I said, "but I doubt it. In fact, I'm not even sure you will keep your commitment to go to A.A. when you do drink."

"I'm not going to drink so it *won't* be a problem."

"Uh-oh. I'm getting you angry, aren't I?"

"I'm not angry."

"You know, I wonder. You said that when Paula was criticizing you, but Martha said that you looked angry. I wonder if you don't know you're angry just like Paula doesn't know she's being critical. I thought you looked angry then, but I don't know you as well as they do. Martha, does he look angry to you?"

Martha hesitated. Her recent behavior had indicated that she would protect Charles rather than his right to drink if she had a choice. I wanted to give her a choice.

"Yes, he looks angry."

"Tina?" She nodded, but her features were freezing up.

"Diana?"

"He looks real pissed."

"Paula?"

"I think he looks angry, too."

"What do you think, Charles?"

"I guess I must be angry," he said, "but I don't know why I should be."

"Any ideas, folks?"

"I think he feels pressured to go to A.A. if he drinks, and he doesn't want to go to A.A.," Paula said.

"Any other ideas?"

"I think Mom's right, and I think he's pissed because you don't think he can do it," Diana said.

"What do you think, Martha?"

"I agree. He feels pressured to go A.A. if he drinks."

"Tina, any thoughts?" She shook her head. It was obvious that she had gone wherever Tinas go when the going gets hairy.

"How did the mindreaders do, Charles?" I asked.

"I think they're right. I think I resented you for saying I was going to drink again, and I feel you are pressuring me about A.A."

"Is it disturbing to you that you didn't know you were angry?"

"Yeah, it is, a little."

"I wonder if you want to learn more about your feelings," I said.

"Yeah, I guess so."

"You know something, though. I'm wondering now whether I'm pressuring you again and you just said that to be nice to me."

"No, I really think I want to."

"Well, we can talk about that later," I said. "I must admit I'm a bit intimidated here because I feel I should finish the subject of drinking, but I get the impression that you really don't want to talk about it."

"No, I'm willing to talk about it," Charles protested.

"The problem I'm having is that you also said you were willing to go to A.A. if you drank, but later realized that you felt pressured. I'm afraid the same thing will happen again." Charles looked confused. "I wonder if you are willing to try an experiment. I wonder if you could look me in the eye and say, 'I don't feel like talking about my drinking right now, and I want you to stop pressuring me.' Are you willing to try that?"

"Okay. I don't feel like talking about my drinking right now, and I want you to stop pressuring me."

"How did that feel?" I asked.

"Okay," Charles said. He wasn't going to make this easy.

"Did it feel right to you?" I pressed.

"I think so," he said. He looked so miserable that I felt really sorry for him.

"Charles, I just realized something. You used to work in Navy Intelligence, didn't you?"

"Yes."

"And they taught you interrogation techniques, didn't they?"

"Yeah." He had gone from miserable to puzzled again.

"Did you actually do interrogations in the service?"

"Yeah."

"Were you good at it?"

"Well, actually they asked me to conduct a seminar for field operatives."

"I thought so. And now you do insurance investigations?"

"Not anymore. I run the department now." He was warming up.

"I guess that could be taken as an indication that you were pretty good at investigating when you were doing it, eh?"

Charles didn't answer, but he was concentrating, getting an inkling of what I was up to. Too late, I hoped.

"In insurance investigations," I went on, "you often have to get people to give you information they don't want to give you, isn't that true?"

"Sometimes."

"How do you go about that?"

"Well, there are lots of different ways." My flattery clearly was not turning his head. I was not going to get a free seminar on interrogation techniques.

"I imagine you folks are wondering what this is all about?" Paula and Diana nodded. Martha, Charles's bodyguard, continued to look vigilant.

"Well, I was wondering why I found myself acting as Charles's agent in setting limits on me. There he sat, while I was busy acting as his attorney, taking care of him as though he was incapable of taking care of himself. Him, a professional interrogator. Charles, I've got to hand it to you. You got me fair and square. I'm completely sincere, Charles, when I say that it's a privilege to work with you. It's no disgrace to be outmaneuvered by a master." Charles smiled disarmingly.

"I wasn't maneuvering," he began. "I really didn't know what was going on."

"I'm impressed by your modesty, Charles," I said, "but it's a little frightening to think that you have me eating out of your hand by not maneuvering. I'd hate to deal with you when you were. I can see how he gets you all stymied," I said to the family. "He's as good as I've ever seen.

"If I guess right, you are going to get me to stop bringing up your drinking and not to hold you to your commitment to go to A.A. when you start to drink again. Am I correct?" The miserable look was back. I felt a fear reaction in my throat and stomach. I didn't know whether I was empathically resonating with Charles or simply feeling my own apprehension.

"I guess I was trying to get you off my drinking, but I don't think I really want you to," Charles said. "Things are so much better when I don't drink. You know, it sounds crazy, but I think I am afraid of things working better."

"What do you mean?" I asked.

"Well, this week was really good. I spent time with the kids, and I had energy to do things. I was more relaxed and productive at the office, and yet I found myself feeling scared at times—you know, like something terrible was going to happen. I used to feel scared like that all the time when I was in the service. You could make a mistake and get somebody killed. You could never feel safe in intelligence work. Now there's no reason to feel that way, but I do. I used drink to make that feeling go away when I was in the service. I guess that's why I didn't want to talk about my drinking. I guess I knew I was planning to drink again. I don't think I want to."

Diana was looking at her father. I asked her, "Diana, do you ever feel that feeling your father was talking about?"

"Oh yeah, all the time. Like when the principal finds out about something heavy and tells you to come in after school, and your gut is in knots all day. Yeah."

"Did you feel it this week?" I asked.

"Maybe, I'm not sure."

"Did anyone else feel scared this week for no good reason?" I pressed. No reply. Puzzled looks all around. The death of a promising young hypothesis. I had speculated that the specter of change in the Cristie family would have sent waves of fear through the entire family, and that Charles was simply resonating with a general feeling.

I tried a different tack. "Charles, I get the impression that you want to stay off booze this week, but you think it will be tough?"

"Yeah, I think so."

"Would it make you feel pressured if I mentioned my friend in A.A. again?"

"Yes, it would, but I think you better ask him to call. I think I'm going to need help."

"Charles," I said, "I wonder if you are at all curious as to what the other people here are feeling about what you just said?"

"Uh, yeah, I am." There was silence. My anxiety sent words for me to say, but I was able to find the resources to shut up.

Diana spoke. "I never thought of you as being scared, Dad. I was always scared of you, and it's weird listening to you talk like that. I'm really glad you're not going to drink. I didn't realize what a difference it made until this week."

Then Paula said, "This is the first time I believed you when you said you were going to stop drinking. I've been married to you all these years and never knew what you felt or thought or anything. I feel like I've been married to a stranger.'' I felt impelled to reframe her statement optimisitically. There will be plenty of time later, I told myself.

Martha said, ''I'm really proud of you, Dad. I'm glad you're going to go to A.A.''

Everyone turned to Tina. ''I love you, Daddy,'' she said and blushed.

''I really admire what you did,'' I said to Charles. ''It takes a lot of courage to undertake a hard job knowing it's going to be a hard job. I'm also glad you shared your feelings with me and your family. It helped me understand you better and to feel closer to you.'' As I looked around, Paula and Diana were nodding their heads. I continued, ''I think you folks are going to have some rough times coming up. When Charles changes the way he functions in the family, everyone is going to have to change, too, and I don't have to tell you that change, even positive change, is difficult. Charles is going to need help, and he's getting it. I think you could all use help as well. Paula, what are my chances of getting you to try an Al-Anon meeting? I have a friend who can call you and take you to a meeting.''

''How can I refuse after Charles has agreed to try A.A.?''

''Girls, have you ever heard of Alateen?'' I asked. ''Alateen is a group for kids who are affected by a parent's drinking. I think it might be of use to you.''

Diana, ever the treatment consumer, nodded her head.

''Good, Diana. Would you be willing to take Tina along with you? Martha, you could try it, too, but you might be a little old for it. You might be more comfortable at Al-Anon with your mother.''

I looked at the clock. Still five minutes left in the session. We had done enough. ''See you all next week,'' I said.

Unlike the week before, I felt full of energy after the session, but even in my euphoria, I realized that there was plenty of hard work to do with the Cristies. Some base had been laid for getting the parents together, but there was still the trauma of Charles's sobriety for them to absorb, assuming that Charles would follow through. I thought Charles looked as though he would follow through, but there are recorded instances of my having been wrong.

As I continued reviewing the session, I came up short. My ego, dangerously inflated, began to lose altitude as I realized that I had sent the Cristies off without reminding them of their homework, the criticism game. Certainly they would forget it after all the fireworks that followed. On reflection, however, this did not seem a tragedy. The criticism game was not the best-thought-out intervention; it had several flaws which might respond well to more time and thought. Meanwhile, I was just as glad that the stress had remained on the family getting help with its drinking problem. The criticism issue had worked insofar as it enabled me to bring up Charles's drinking into a context in which Paula was being criticized and Charles was the injured party.

I never fail to be amazed at the facility with which I can justify not broaching the subject of drinking to an alcoholic family. Here, for example, Charles was not drinking and had vowed to go to A.A. if he did. Everyone was happy, and Charles was moving into a more powerful position in the family. Bringing up the subject of Charles's drinking could be seen as undermining Charles by calling attention to past failures and casting doubt on his resolve and his word, weakening his family's faith in him and his faith in himself. When things are going well, do not mess with them, right?

Wrong. It is important to be extremely suspicious of any reason not to mention drinking to an alcoholic family. Most alcoholic families follow the rule of not mentioning drinking when the drinker is present, and family rules tend to be communicated to outsiders in a subtle but powerful manner. While it is obvious that this rule has not served the family well, a therapist can easily find himself unconsciously accepting it.

In the case of the Cristies, I have no idea how this rule was communicated to me, or even whether it was all my issue, but

I do know that only by consciously riding herd on myself was I able to keep focusing on the drinking. Most therapists I have supervised have experienced similar difficulties. It would be enlightening some day to analyze videotapes of alcoholic family interviews second by second to see what changes in expression, movement, or other behaviors occur when the subject of drinking looms. My guess is that observations will have to get down to the level of breathing patterns, voice prints, muscle tone, pulse, face-color patterns before anything significant will emerge. Long training is required to bring changes on this level to consciousness, but almost everyone responds to them unconsciously. (Bandler and Grinder discuss this in the *Structure of Magic,* Vol. II.) But no matter how the Cristies enforced their rule, it was my job to break it. It is much better to deal with a relapse before it happens than to have to cut through the added growth of guilt and defensiveness after it happens.

There are a number of reasons why I usually use the tactic of confidently predicting a relapse in this situation. First, as has been discussed, it mobilizes the forces of opposition where I want them—on the side of sobriety. Second, it follows a rule best expressed by a fine strategic therapist, Carter Umbarger, Ph.D., who said, ''A therapist is always safe in predicting disaster. If it doesn't happen, the family can feel a real sense of accomplishment; if it does, at least they know they have a smart therapist.''

Charles was very skillful at countermaneuvering me into the untenable position of the ''voice of sobriety.'' I found myself quickly in the position of arguing with Charles about a subject in which he had all the data: his feelings. To extricate myself from an argument I had to lose, I called in the family. This move had two advantages: it tested where the family was at the moment by giving each member a chance to vote for or against Charles's denial, and it put the conflict in the family rather than between Charles and myself. Had a significant portion of the family supported Charles's denial of anger, I would have apologized for overinterpreting and proceeded on the assumption that Charles was comfortable. The actual vote was, in my opinion, interpreted by Charles as permission to be angry and express his opposition directly. When I pushed that farther than was comfortable, he reverted to the oppressed little boy role, and I began to feel I was being abusive.

In countering, I reminded Charles and the family of the fact that he was indeed a competent adult and a master at the little game we were playing. It was clear to me, however, that the person who most needed reminding was the therapist.

The whole family made the most of their opportunity to give Charles a clear message about his drinking, and Charles responded by rising to the occasion. One danger in working with alcoholic families is to become complacent at moments like this. The family seems mobilized for sobriety. The drinker has a dry week behind him and has agreed to go to A.A. I have permission to turn my cheerfully persistent A.A. contact loose on Charles and am stepping up the pressure to get other family members into self-help groups as well.

It is useful to remember here that this family has spent its entire existence organized around Charles's drunkenness, and although everyone is overjoyed at Charles's resolve to change, the family has few skills appropriate to living with a sober, competent Charles. A therapist can expect that a family in this situation will find itself behaving in ways which will make it easy for the drinker to return to drinking. It is important to keep in mind that this does not mean the family wants the alcoholic to drink, but only that a system will behave so as to reject change and restabilize itself. With this in mind, I entered the next session.

One look at Paula's set jaw and I could see that the Cristies had dismounted from the "pink cloud" they had been riding the previous week. This was further confirmed by the faces of Diana and Tina. Martha also looked grim, and Charles immediately settled into his hangdog posture. Energy began to drain as I surveyed this disgruntled crew.

"I'm afraid to ask you how things are going," I began. "What's going on?"

"We were all fighting in the car," Diana said.

"What was the fight about?"

"Me, as usual. Mom is all over my case for nothing, as usual."

"Nothing?" said Paula. "You call failing Spanish nothing? The one saving grace through all this was that Diana was able to keep her grades up. Now even that's collapsing, and when I try to discuss it with her, she's rude and insulting!"

"Discuss! You jumped all over me without even asking what's going on. You don't even know what you're talking about!"

"I'm talking about that notice that came in the mail. That's what I'm talking about. You hang out with your junkie friends when you should be studying, that's what I'm talking about!" Paula rose to the bait like a trout.

In the old days I would have calmly questioned Diana about the notice, thereby showing her parents how a competent expert handles an adolescent. I have not found the results of such methods very impressive, however. "What do you think is going on, Charles?" I asked.

"I didn't see the notice. I got home just in time to come here." I thought I detected a trace of defensiveness.

"The notice came yesterday," Paula said. "By the time you came home from that meeting of yours, I was asleep. Not that you're interested."

"I've been spending more time with the kids recently." More defense.

"For years he sat in that den and drank his head off," Paula went on. "Now he finally stops drinking and spends all his time at those A.A. meetings. He might as well still be drinking for the use he is to his family." Charles stared at the floor, forearms on knees. Where had I seen that posture before?

Charles seemed to be accumulating grievance coupons so that he could cash them in for a drink. Paula was practically saying that his grand sacrifice for the family was not appreciated and that she resented A.A. As I began formulating my countermove, Martha spoke up.

"That's not fair, Mom. Dad's really been trying." I decided to move before she further infantilized her father by standing up for him.

"Do you really think *your father* needs you to defend him? As I recall, this is the same guy who maneuvered me into shutting myself up last week. Now he's maneuvered your mother into practically telling him not to go to A.A. meetings, and you think he needs *your* help?" Charles didn't look up.

"Paula, I support your not tiptoeing around Charles, but I don't see why you are letting him off the hook and not demanding that he deal with Diana. Do you enjoy it that much that you want to keep it all to yourself?"

"Certainly not, but Charles would never help me with the children, and I guess I don't expect him to."

"Charles supervises fifty-two people at work. I would imagine he is up to dealing with a sixteen-year-old girl about a Spanish grade or anything else for that matter. What do you think, Charles?"

"I guess I am," Charles said. His mouth said yes, but the rest of him said no.

"Well, there's no question that you can if you want to, but you don't look as though you want to. I wonder if you're afraid Paula will resent it if you move in on her job. I wouldn't be surprised, with the way this family protects each other."

Charles looked up. "Protects each other? What do you mean?"

"Diana knows her mother is mad at you, so she protects you by drawing her fire. Martha tries to protect you by defending you to Paula. Paula protects you by not asking you to help her with Diana, or maybe she's protecting Diana. You protect Paula by acting like a zombie rather than moving into her territory. There is no question in my mind that you people are watching out for each other every second. Even Tina protects everyone by keeping her mouth shut, because she knows just what's going on."

"Well, I *am* reluctant to step in with the kids. And Paula usually criticizes me when I try."

"What do you mean?" said Paula, sounding genuinely surprised.

"Well, you just implied that I hadn't seen the notice because I only cared about my meetings."

"I didn't mean that."

"Charles, do you know whether or not Paula really wants you to deal with Diana?" I interrupted.

"No."

"What about it, Paula?"

"Yes, I do. Diana drives me to my wit's end, and I need help."

"Do you believe her, Charles?" I asked.

"Yes."

"What are you going to do when you start to deal with Diana and Paula criticizes you? Old habits die hard, and sometimes I don't even think she knows when she's doing it," I persisted.

"I'll point it out and ask her to stop," Charles said.

"What will you do then?" I asked Paula.

"I'll stop."

"Don't make any rash promises," I cautioned. "You don't have to bend over backwards to be nice to him, but I think you guys can work it out after a little friction. Anyhow, why don't we give it a try. Why don't you find out what's happening in Spanish, Charles?"

"Yeah. What's going on, Diana?"

"Nothing," Diana mumbled.

"Nothing? Then why are we getting notices?"

"None of your fucking business." It was Diana's usual crescendo. "Two weeks off the booze and he's 'Father Knows Best.' Shit!"

"Listen, Diana," Charles said. "I know you're angry at me, and perhaps you have a right to be, but you better never talk to me like that again. You can save your 'fucks' and 'shits' for your friends. I don't use that language with you, and you won't use it with me either. Now what's happening in Spanish?"

"The notice doesn't mean anything," Diana said in a normal tone of voice. "I was sick for a test and forgot to come in to make it up. I got a ninety on the only test I did take. But he gave me a zero on the other one. I know the stuff okay."

"What are you going to do about the test you missed?" Charles again.

"I'll make it up next week."

"When you do, I'd like you to ask your teacher for a note to let me know you're all square."

"Oh Dad, that's humiliating. Mr. *Greer,* I need a note for my parents because they don't believe me!"

"You're damned right we don't believe you," Paula said. "You always lie."

"Now who's swearing?" Diana shouted in triumph.

"Don't you change the subject," Paula shot back. "I'm going to call your Spanish teacher tomorrow and find out if you're telling the truth." Charles met my eye and grinned.

"Do you want to handle this yourself after all?" he asked Paula.

"No. She gets me mad when she's so self-righteous."

"I know, she gets to me, too. Diana, I'm afraid I'll have to insist on the note, unless you'd rather have me call Mr. Greer?"

"No, I'll get a note," Diana said, subdued now.

"You know," I said, "I wonder if Diana is betting that you won't follow up and that the whole thing will blow over?"

"I hope she isn't," Charles said. "I'm assuming that she is telling the truth, but if I don't have a note by next Friday, she'll be grounded for the weekend."

"Does that seem fair to you, Paula?" I asked.

"Yes, very fair. I think Charles handled that very well."

"I think you both did. That was pretty good teamwork considering that you just started. Diana, you are going to have to keep testing them until you are sure that they can come through for you. Do you think you can do that without putting yourself in danger?" Diana was silent.

"Paula, one more thing," I said. "How many A.A. meetings can Charles attend before you begin to feel abandoned?"

"Oh, I don't know, he can go to all the meetings he wants. I said that before because I was cross."

"No, really, if he's out all the time, you are going to feel like it's all on your shoulders. How many meetings would make sense from your point of view?"

"I guess about three a week," she said, after considering the question.

"Is that enough for you, Charles?" I asked.

"I suppose so, but the guys at the program say that when you're just getting started, you should make a lot of meetings—five, six, seven a week."

"How long do you figure you will need that many?" I asked.

"Oh, a couple of weeks," Charles said.

"Paula, would you be willing to let Charles attend up to seven meetings a week for a month if he is willing to cut back to three after that?" I asked.

"Sure."

"I'm afraid I pushed you into this," I said.

"Well, you did, but I know that A.A. is important, and I'm so glad Charles is doing it. I'm happy for him to go to as many meetings as he needs."

"Charles," I said, "I'm afraid you are going to be considerate of Paula and not make as many meetings as you need. Will you really take advantage of her offer?"

"Yes, I will."

As the session ended, I felt a quiet excitement. It looked as if the Cristies were starting to realign themselves along more workable lines. I knew it was far too early for unbridled optimism; Charles was barely two weeks dry and scarcely tested. I wondered what would have happened if Diana had answered his firm limit setting with the dramatic escalation of which I knew her to be capable. The fact that she didn't choose to was encouraging. Charles and the family would have more time without booze to prepare to meet her challenge. So far, in spite of my injunction, everyone was treating Charles gingerly. This was a mixed blessing; he was protected from the powerless feelings that might make drinking more attractive but also weakened as a parent. Parents need to be able to stand up to stress, especially parents of an adolescent like Diana. A.A. simply says, "First things first." Stop the drinking first, then start to see what else might need to be done. The father position wasn't going to score many points if Charles started drinking again.

Alcoholics Anonymous is a potent ally for both alcoholics and therapists. It is designed to avoid traps which often render professionals helpless. It is therefore important for all helping professionals to have some mental model of how A.A. works.

When a supervisor insisted that I attend A.A. meetings, I was resentful but could find no way to refute his argument that a therapist who refers people to A.A. should understand A.A. It took some time for me to develop an idea of the A.A. process, and just as A.A. traditions state that everyone must work his or her own program, my understanding of A.A. is my own, and there are an infinite number of other valid ways of understanding A.A.

A prospective A.A. member finds himself or herself sitting on a folding chair in a church basement or school auditorium filled with men and women of varying ages and styles of dress. Typically the prospective member will be greeted but not crowded. The atmosphere is sincere, relaxed, and unpretentious.

Many members radiate the kind of undifferentiated friendliness that might be associated with righteousness or religion. Our prospective person may begin to feel in danger of being preached at. Many alcoholics have a knack of drawing preaching behavior from a wide variety of people, so their senses are quick to spot a potential preaching situation. The opening prayer, therefore, might not put the prospective member at ease. Our "pigeon" is becoming certain that it was a mistake to come to the meeting.

The first speaker begins, and the churchlike atmosphere dissipates slightly. The speaker is unlikely to be an orator. Both ecclesiastical pomp and barroom grandiosity are rare. The story tends to be simple and factual. The speaker introduces himself or herself by first name and adds the label, "I'm an alcoholic." Then there is usually an account of the speaker's relationship to alcohol. The metamorphosis of alcohol from trusted friend to treacherous intimate to obligating burden is outlined. The story recounts tragedy, shame, defensiveness, loss, and hopelessness. The sense of doom lifts with the discovery of A.A., the realization that one has a treatable disease. The stories typically end on the theme of struggle, hope, increasing confidence and self-respect, moments of joy and success. Often deep gratitude to A.A. and its members and a self-warning against complacency close the talk.

And then another speaker. The content varies, but the process of increasing hopelessness and self-hate to A.A. to increasing joy and hope unify the stories. The room is stuffy and smoky, the speakers' stories become predictable. The voices drone. Trance begins to set in. The conscious mind is no longer alert enough to pounce on every point which proves the new member is unalterably different from the speaker and therefore doomed to a drunkard's grave. Our prospect relaxes as messages / slogans are repeated with the same wording. "The Disease of Alcoholism." "First Things First." "Easy Does It." "Live and Let Live." "Let Go and Let God." In a trance state these simple slogans stick to the mind like burrs.

The members are friendly and accepting and stress their sameness rather than their differences. The man with the five-hundred-dollar suit is an alcoholic just like the attractive young woman, just like our prospective member, who may begin to realize that their very presence defines alcoholism as a solvable problem. Our member cannot be isolated here by being a one-member set of "worthless, irresponsible drunk." Here almost everyone has done the same, or worse.

Yet on a more subtle level, the message is confusing. Let go—surrender—turn over your will to a higher power—this is certainly not how people, particularly American males, are taught to solve problems.

Our member conceptualizes the problem as weakness—not

being strong enough, not being self-reliant enough, not fighting hard enough. Yet here are people who have apparently "beaten" alcoholism talking about accepting defeat, giving up the struggle, "Letting go and letting God." Our bored, entranced prospect is confused, with no conscious model to organize this information.

Many hypnotic techniques combine an environment of drowsy comfort and confusion. The master hypnotherapist Milton Erickson taught a "confusion technique" in which he would present a rush of familiar ideas in unfamiliar or rapidly changing contexts so that his subject would have an expectation of understanding but, as the patter danced just ahead of conscious attempts to understand, would become confused or entranced.

When people feel secure in their understanding of what is going on, they are relatively closed to new information. Confusion and insecurity tend to make outside suggestions more welcome. A.A. offers suggestions in an atmosphere of comfort and drowsiness tempered by subtle confusion. There are direct suggestions, i.e., "Keep It Simple," "One Day at a Time." But perhaps even more powerful are the suggestions made by implication. Possibly the most important is that there is hope. Almost all alcoholics are positive there is no hope for them. The members of A.A. belie that by being like the prospective member—but being happy and sober. The seeming simplicity of the slogans imply the answer is simple, yet there is this confusing message of "letting go." The implication of this is that the "pigeon" must find a new model of understanding self, alcohol, and power to get the "simple" message. A.A. is not quite as simple as it looks.

In a brilliant essay "The Cybernetics of Self: Toward a Theory of Alcoholism," Gregory Bateson makes explicit the profound wisdom of the A.A. program. He sees the alcoholic locked in a struggle with alcohol. The outcome of the struggle is predictable—alcohol always wins, leaving its opponent sick, shame-ridden, and vanquished. Every strategy the alcoholic tries ends the same way. The alcoholic is caught up in the struggle, and the process of a struggle often transcends its content. We have all seen opponents in a bitter argument switch sides with regard to content, arguing both sides with equal vehemence. These embarrassing incidents can be explained by the notion that the fact of the argument was primary and the content secondary. The fight is the thing.

Thus if the alcoholic adopts the tactic of defeating alcohol by not drinking, the struggle is suspended. As *not* drinking becomes easier, the sense of struggle becomes dimmed. How can one keep fighting alcohol now?

The answer, of course, is not to avoid the opponent, but to engage it on one's own terms. The alcoholic can only do battle with alcohol by drinking in a controlled manner. By definition the alcoholic, in spite of some possible initial success, must necessarily lose this battle and wind up again sick, shame-ridden, and vanquished. This pattern repeats over and over with the price of defeat rising constantly.

This may explain A.A.'s insistence that the battle must stop. Once we admit defeat, we need make no more ventures into enemy territory. We can stop and stay stopped securely defeated by alcohol, thus free to stop the struggle.

The whole structure of A.A. reflects the implied message, "Avoid Power Struggles." A.A.'s wisdom recognizes that the problem for many alcoholics at the level of content is alcohol, but at the level of process the problem is symmetric power struggles.The alcoholic must avoid power struggles in general—must "Live and Let Live."

A.A. has no hierarchy. No presidents, no elections, no titles. The chair of a meeting is a rotating obligation, as likely occupied by a new member as one with twenty years sobriety. No one in A.A. is an authority, so there is no authority to battle, to placate, to disappoint. Each member owns his or her program and attends to work on his or her own personal recovery. The process of helping others recover is explicitly a part of one's own recovery. The twelfth step in A.A.'s twelve-step program enjoins members to carry the message of spiritual awakening to other alcoholics and to live by A.A. principles. This means that the alcoholic's primary job is his own recovery and that helping others is a means toward that end. This helps avoid the trap of A.A. members struggling with prospective members. If the "pigeon" won't accept the program, then he hasn't hit bottom yet, and A.A. members will quietly remind him that the program is there when wanted and continue to go about the business of their own recovery. There are no A.A. counselors, only A.A. members.

This may explain why some A.A. members find the going so difficult when they become professional alcoholism counselors. The moment they accept compensation or a professional role, they forgo the protection so carefully woven into the fabric of the A.A. program. They are now working for the agency and the client, not themselves. They are responsible for results. They must document their work, thus losing the protection of anonymity for themselves and their clients. As professional counselors, they become authority figures against whom clients can act out. The passive tactics of A.A. are inappropriate in professional settings. A professional is responsible to *do something*. To become effective counselors, these A.A. members must learn strategies which do not depend on the protection afforded by A.A. traditions.

The stress A.A. places on a "higher power" is the single aspect of the program most difficult for many alcoholics to accept. God is linked with religion and religion with self-righteous judgmental disapproval in the minds of many alcoholics (among others). Yet a higher power is absolutely central to the effectiveness of the program. A higher power is a safe authority from whom one can accept help without initiating power struggles with human beings. A higher power can take over the battle with alcohol that the alcoholic must abandon, can be asked for forgiveness without fear of recrimination, can be asked for love when one does not feel very lovable.

In order to make a higher power available to new members, A.A. is flexible in its definition of the term. One's higher power can be any concept that seems to work, and is not necessarily linked to God or to a divine entity. One A.A. member told me that in the early days his higher power was a toilet bowl because he had spent considerable time kneeling in front of it each day. Other A.A. members who overheard this comment expressed appreciation for the man's humor, and felt he was expressing wisdom rather than blasphemy. Of course the concept of a higher power often becomes richer and more complex with a member's maturing sobriety. The steps become more frankly spiritual as the member becomes more sophisticated in the use of his or her higher power.

Many alcoholics are susceptible to the myth that they must perfect their personalities in order to remain sober. This all-or-nothing system makes a step-by-step recovery program impossible. A.A. wisely identifies this all-or-nothing rule as an aspect of alcoholism. Alcoholics are given the task of asking for God to remove their defects in character, thus releasing them from the battle with their own personalities. God is the way out of power struggles, and power struggles are the process level of the disease of alcoholism. This is one reason why professional alcoholism counselors who are not always afforded God's protection must understand power and the traps it sets. This is why the first part of this book stressed techniques of avoiding power struggles and utilizing them in the aid of recovery.

Thus in the case of the Cristie family the therapist must recognize the potential power struggle at this point of treatment. The family is in crisis. It is in the process of enduring a change which renders many of its familiar coping mechanisms irrelevant. One can draw the analogy of a trip to a foreign country with strange language and customs. The long-anticipated adventure is exciting but frightening. Fluency in one's own language and customs is irrelevant. One cannot feel competent. There is a strong temptation to regress to old strategies of coping, such as a childlike dependency on people perceived as competent in the unfamiliar environment.

As stated above, the Cristie family was in crisis. In the session, the family moved to alleviate stress by returning to familiar patterns: Charles as peripheral, incompetent, and defensive; Paula as central, angry, and helpless; Diana as provocative and misbehaving; Martha as protector of Father and attacker of

Diana; and Tina as absent. All my moves were aimed at blocking this response.

These moves were successful in that the Cristies returned to their new pattern with a competent Charles and a cooperative, supportive Paula. Martha was blocked from intruding into the parental team by protecting her father, and Diana was faced by two active parents who agreed on what to do. As rewarding as this all might be in the abstract, it is putting enormous pressure on every member of the family. They are all living with strangers whose bodies resemble people they have known all their lives. This is an archetypical nightmare expressed by tales of demonic possession and in movies like *The Body Snatchers*. I did not expect the next session to be uneventful.

The day before that session I received a message from Charles that he was canceling. Paula was too ill to attend. Reluctant to let this stand, I called back immediately. Diana answered the phone. She sounded happy to hear from me and launched into an anecdote about school. I asked to speak to one of her parents, but she said they were both out. This was odd, given Paula's illness. I asked how everyone was, and Diana said, "Fine." I resisted the temptation to question her further, and left a message. While I might have received useful information from Diana, I felt it was unwise to question an acting-out adolescent about the antics of the parents I was trying to place in charge of her.

At nine that evening, when my call had still not been returned, I dialed the Cristies' number. After several rings Paula answered. She sounded sleepy, and I asked if I had awakened her. She said I hadn't. I asked how she was, and she said that she wasn't feeling all that well, and then she giggled. I asked if they were planning to come the next evening and she said she didn't know. She was starting to sound more normal. I asked if Charles was in, but Paula said he was at an A.A. meeting and wasn't expected back till late. I said that I hoped she felt better, but that it was very, very important for the family to come to the session whether Paula could make it or not. I also told her that

I would call Charles at work the next day. After a long pause, she said she would tell him.

Something was wrong with the conversation, but I couldn't quite place what. Why had I said I would call Charles at work? I was treating Paula like an irresponsible teenager. Why had Diana seemed so glad to hear from me? The last session certainly had not done anything to endear me to her. I decided that these mysteries would keep until tomorrow.

My phone call to Charles the following morning did little to enlighten me. It was clear that Paula had not told him of my call. Charles said that Paula was not feeling well, and that they weren't planning to come. I told him that I had told Paula that it was extremely important that we not miss a week at this stage of treatment and that I wanted to meet the family with or without Paula. After some hesitation, he said he was worried about leaving Paula alone. I asked if he could find a friend to stay with her. After more hesitation, he said that they would find a way to come. In a cheery voice I said that I was looking forward to seeing them.

I was just learning then—and am even clearer now—about the value of a therapist *insisting* on what he feels to be necessary and not negotiating. In *Techniques of Family Therapy* by Jay Haley and Lynn Hoffman, Carl Whitaker demonstrates how he insists on the unit of treatment he thinks appropriate and then responds to resistance by escalating his demands. I remember reading that and wishing I were a master so that I could be high-handed, too. I have since come to feel that until I become a master, I can practice by acting like one. Therapy is hard enough without compromising on essentials. I have found that a firm insistence about issues which a therapist feels are pivotal to successful treatment will usually be respected by the family.

When Paula arrived five minutes before the session was to start, I realized that I was not particularly surprised to see her. Her manner, however, gave me pause. Her face was blank and slack, and her eyes seemed fixed on some far distant point. She nodded absently in my general direction and sank into a chair, utilizing much more of the seat than usual. Diana and Martha followed, talking and giggling in a way which immediately struck me as unauthentic.

Then Charles arrived with Tina shadowing him. He looked agitated and worried, his eyes darting to Paula and then to me. He sat down on the edge of a chair. Tina pulled up a chair next to his and sat almost—but not quite—touching him.

Before I could think of a question, Charles spoke. "Well, it's been quite a week." I waited, but he did not elaborate.

"What do you mean?" I asked. Silence. "What do you mean quite a week?" I repeated.

"Maybe Paula should tell you about it," Charles said.

Diana and Martha began to watch their mother as if she had suddenly changed colors. Paula's expression, however, had not changed from the catatonic mask she had walked in with. Then a single tear rolled down her cheek. Other than that, there was no sound or movement. I noticed Tina's eyes had filled.

"Do you want to say anything, Paula?" I asked gently, trying to time my breathing to hers. The tears started coming faster. She sobbed—a long pause—another sob, then, "I don't know what's happening to me." Another long teary silence. My gut was in a knot. I don't know how much was my own consternation at Paula acting so un-Paulalike and how much was resonance with the surprise and distress of the other family members.

"Mom's been drinking," Diana blurted out.

Charles spoke quickly. "I came home from my meeting Monday night and Paula was upstairs asleep. Usually she waits up, but not always. The girls were still watching T.V. in the den.

"Anyway," Charles continued, "I talked to Diana about school for a few minutes and then went upstairs. Paula was on the bed with her clothes still on. Her breathing sounded peculiar. I still hadn't figured it out. I went into the bathroom and there was some vomit on the toilet seat and the toilet hadn't been flushed. The first thing I thought was, Diana's done it again. I was furious. And then I looked over at Paula. She was motionless, but tears were dripping off her chin. I leaned over and handed her a box of tissues, and I realized she was asleep. face.

"So help me God, even with the smell it didn't occur to me she was drunk. I haven't seen her take more than one drink in a night in twenty-five years. Then I saw the bottle on the bedside table. It was a brand of scotch I used to drink years ago—half empty. I couldn't figure where she got it. I had thrown all the booze out three weeks ago, when I quit drinking "

"You hid that bottle years ago. I knew where it was," Paula said in a surprisingly normal voice.

Charles went on. "I was worried about her breathing and decided to try to wake her. Sometimes, when I was in the service, we would have to wake somebody up when they were drunk. I got her up and walked her to our bathroom. I started wiping her face with a cold wet towel. Nothing happened for a long time. Then she suddenly woke up and cursed me with words I didn't even think she knew."

"I could hear her from downstairs," Diana said. "I couldn't believe it was Mom saying that stuff."

"Anyway, she passed out again. I got her clothes off and put her to bed. After cleaning up the bathroom, I went to sleep. Paula was still asleep when I left that morning. I called a few times during the day but didn't get an answer. Finally about four in the afternoon Diana answered and said I'd better get home. I left as soon as I could. As I was coming up the walk I could hear her cursing and shouting. I asked Paula where Tina was, and she said she was hiding with Diana. When I told her to leave the kids alone, she cursed me again. I grabbed her around the arms and took her into our bedroom."

"I got home then," said Martha. "At first I thought it was an animal crying, the sound was so strange. When I saw it was Mom, I got really scared. I thought she was having a breakdown."

As soon as Martha had stopped talking, Charles rushed on. "After Paula stopped crying, she just curled up in my arms and fell asleep. I carried her to the bed, and then I called your office to cancel tonight.''

"How come?'' I asked.

"I don't know. I guess I didn't want to embarrass Paula. I just know that it seemed important to cancel the appointment.''

Paula's face seemed inhabited now; her body was more relaxed than I had ever seen it. "What's going on, Paula?'' I asked, with a smile. "I don't know,'' she said. "Monday night Charles worked late and went straight to his A.A. meeting. Martha was working late, and Diana was studying with a friend. Only Tina was home. I started to get some supper for Tina and me when I suddenly thought of this bottle that Charles had hidden when he was really drinking. I'd been afraid to throw it away, so I hid it in a canister. I don't know what made me remember it, but I remember how happy I was when the canister felt heavy. I poured a little into a glass and tasted it, and then I poured some orange juice in and put ice in it.''

"Scotch and orange juice?'' said Charles.

"I just kept pouring and drinking. After a while Tina came into the kitchen and said she was hungry. I told her to leave me alone.''

"That's not what you said!'' Tina looked wounded.

"I'm sorry, honey,'' Paula said. "I didn't mean whatever I said.'' Tina nodded, and Paula went on. "I took the bottle upstairs. I remember being surprised that I could drink right out of the bottle. When I woke up in the morning, everyone was gone, and I felt pretty bad. I had a headache, and my mouth was so dry. I took some aspirin, but it didn't help much. . . . The bottle was still on the bedside table. It was half-empty, and I remember thinking that Charles must have had some and feeling guilty. The whiskey smelled awful, but I put some orange juice in it, and I could drink it.

"When Tina and Diana came home, I tried to act normal, but Diana said I was drunk, and I told her to mind her own business. She gave me some back talk and we started to argue.

She and Tina ran into Diana's room and locked the door. That's when Charles came in.''

"We were in there for an hour before Dad came home," Diana said.

"Do you remember talking to me on the phone last night?" I asked.

"Sort of. Like in a dream," Paula said.

Charles broke in. "I decided to go to A.A. anyway last night. I threw out the rest of the booze and told the kids to stay next door till I got home. I told them to say Paula was sick and they didn't want to bother her. Diana and Tina stayed there this afternoon until I got home." Charles looked at me expectantly. They very much needed me to do something; they were all very shaken, Paula most of all.

I let the suspense build. Anxiety and anticipation help people to be more attentive and open to new ideas.

"Paula," I said quietly, "I'm sure you think you're going crazy. After all these years of living with an alcoholic, you probably think the virus has infected you, and now you've got it worse than Charles ever did."

Paula nodded. Everyone looked grave.

"Well, that may be true, but I doubt it. In fact, I think this whole thing is a brilliant stroke on the part of your unconscious mind to keep the family stable. You realized that when Charles quit drinking after all these years, you and the girls would still see him as an uncaring, incompetent drunk, A.A. or no A.A. One thing you learn in this business is to respect the creativity of people's unconscious minds. The unconscious can solve problems that people don't even consciously know they have. I don't know whether you've heard the story of the kids who ate paint. The doctors thought these kids were crazy. They would peel paint off windowsills and doors and eat it—white paint. Everyone thought they were nuts. Especially the kids. They eat paint—everybody tells them not to—it's bad for you— it's weird—there's something wrong with you. Can you imagine having an uncontrollable urge to eat paint in spite of what everybody says, in spite of what you keep telling yourself? It's crazy, but you just keep doing it.''

I had been timing my voice to Paula's breathing, and at this point I looked intensely into her eyes. Her eyes were fixed on mine—unblinking. This time I hoped it was trance—not a return to catatonia.

I had started to talk about the family problem before I launched into my tale of the amazing paint eaters of North America. I was hoping her unconscious would make links between her problem and theirs, but I was not going to leave it to chance. Milton Erickson had the uncanny knack of perceiving unconscious process—sometimes working entirely in metaphor and never making explicit what he was getting at. And this was what I was attempting to do.

"Finally some doctor got interested in the problem of these crazy paint-eating kids. He took them all in for tests. Can you guess what he found?

"He found that they all had calcium deficiencies. Kids need a lot of calcium to build bones. They weren't getting enough. Their conscious minds didn't know that, but some part of them knew—some part deep inside. And that part of them gave them an urge to eat paint, which contained a high level of calcium. Their unconscious minds had solved a problem they didn't even know they had—but it sure made them look crazy in the process. Now . . . what's the problem you didn't know you had, but you solved anyway?''

Paula still looked entranced; her head nodded slightly. Did that mean she got it? Would that have been enough for Erickson?

"Just as a child has a wonderfully intimate knowledge of his or her growing body, a mother has intimate knowledge of her family and its needs. This family has needed a father for a long time. Charles proved he has all the skills for the job, but he proved it to a bunch of insurance executives. He never proved it here. Here he was an irresponsible drunk. Highballs and T.V. All of you were hypnotized to believe that's what he really was. Even he thought so. Nobody here would let him be a father. So your unconscious developed a plan—and you developed a craving for alcohol—one you had never experienced before—you never had hope before. But now Charles is ready to be the father this family needs. So you get drunk and force him to take care of all of you, and how does he do it— brilliantly, that's how.''

Charles seemed to be in trance, too—so did Diana. Martha was concentrating, but I could see her swallowing and shifting her eyes. Tina looked bored.

''You never, never would trust your family, Paula, to anyone unless you were sure that person would come through. Now everyone in the family knows they can count on having a father when the chips are down. Paula, your unconscious moved this from a family with one drunk and one parent to a family with two drunks and two parents! Now that you showed Charles what a good father he is, maybe he'll take you to A.A. and teach you how to be a sober drunk.''

I find myself inclined to agree with those who believe that all effective therapy is hypnotic in that it initiates a change in unconscious structure which is evidenced by a spontaneous change in attitude, perception, or behavior. My monologue was an attempt to help the Cristies respond to an apparent disaster as a triumphant breakthrough.

I started by feeding back to them my perception of their experience: a frightening change in the tower of strength on whom they all depended. I then asserted that this perception was wrong and that the perceived disaster was in fact a brilliant solution to a problem. I hinted at the problem—everyone's mistrust of Charles—but gave no hint of how it was related. All of this was designed to create an atmosphere of confusion and anxiety and with it a need for resolution. In the same way, dropping one shoe focuses attention on the anticipated sound of the other shoe falling or the dominant chord urges us to listen for the resolution.

Having created this tension, I launched into my tale of the paint-eating children. My hope was that the tension would urge

the Cristies to find a message in the story. Like Paula, the
children had ingested a poisonous substance. Like Paula, the
children's unconscious minds were solving a problem they did
not even know they had. Like Paula, the children needed
someone to show them that their apparently crazy behavior
was meeting a real need.

After the session just recounted, Paula's drinking stopped.
She actually went to two A.A. meetings with Charles, stating,
"It's the only way I'll get to see him." He got an A.A. spon-
sor and cut back to three meetings a week.

Diana continued to do well in school. There were no more
drug incidents. I predicted that she would act out in order to
test the new family alignment, but so far she has disappointed
me.

Martha didn't say much in the last two sessions, which was
not surprising. Tina did laugh at a joke I told.

About a year after treatment stopped, I got an envelope from
the Cristies with a picture of Charles blowing out the candle
of his first anniversary cake at A.A. and an announcement of
Martha's engagement. There was no news of Diana. I heard
nothing about her until many years later, when I received a
picture of her graduation from college. She majored in psy-
chology.

I've used the Cristies to communicate the subjective experience of working with a fairly typical alcoholic family. I
attempted to expose the pulleys and wires behind the therapy,
hoping to render it less mysterious but at the risk of making it
seem extremely complex, with analyses of power states, presentation of techniques of indirect hypnotic communication,
and multilevel discussions of therapeutic strategies and tactics.

A man who supervised me for three instructive years, Joel
Jay Rogge, J.D., D.D., Ed.D., once told me that the way to
treat alcoholics and their families is to love them. One must
not expect that they will make this easy, and can anticipate
that they will work hard to convince us they are unlovable. He

stressed that one must not love them in spite of this but because of it.

One way of looking at the moves and techniques discussed in this book is to see them as ways to depotentiate the strategies that individuals or families use to avoid or reject love. Alcoholics (and many others) do not feel worthy of love and therefore fear and mistrust anyone who might offer it. The techniques offered here are attempts to circumvent this barrier from one angle, as the twelve steps of the A.A. program attempt to circumvent it from another angle. One hopes that both can help to counter ploys the alcoholic uses to remain rejected and unlovable, and to build self-respect so that it is more possible to give and receive love.

Alcoholics explore the dark side of self for all of us. They therefore provide us with a unique opportunity to practice love and forgiveness. Learning to forgive is a truly healing and maturing experience. Sharing the process of recovery with a family enables therapists to join them in learning compassion, for ourselves as well as for them—making us all more whole.

BIBLIOGRAPHY

ARTICLES

Bateson, Gregory; Weakland, John; Jackson, Don D.; and Haley, Jay. "Toward a Theory of Schizophrenia." *Behavioral Science,* October 1956, pp. 251–264.

Brown, Elizabeth, and Hawley, Nancy. "Children of Alcoholics: The Use of Group Treatment." *Journal of Social Casework,* Vol. 62, No. 1, January 1981.

BOOKS

Bandler, Richard, and Grinder, John. *Structure of Magic,* Volume II. Palo Alto, California: Science & Behavior Books, 1976.

Berne, Eric. *Games People Play.* New York: Ballantine, 1978.

Greenberg, Joanne (Hannah Green). *I Never Promised You a Rose Garden.* New York: Holt, Rinehart & Winston, 1964.

Haley, Jay. *Strategies of Psychotherapy.* New York: Grune & Stratton, c / o Academic Press, 1963.

Haley, Jay. *Uncommon Therapy.* New York: W. W. Norton & Co., 1973.

Haley, Jay, and Hoffman, Lynn. *Techniques of Family Therapy.* New York: Basic Books, 1968.

McClelland, David, et al. *The Drinking Man.* New York: Free Press, 1972.

Minuchin, Salvador. *Families of the Slums.* New York: Basic Books, 1967.

Napier, Augustus Y., and Whitaker, Carl. *The Family Crucible.* New York: Harper & Row, 1978.

Palazzoli, Mara Selvini. *Paradox and Counterparadox.* New York: Jason Aronson, 1978.

Rosenthal, Robert, with Jacobson, Lenore. *Pygmalion in the Classroom.* New York: Holt, Rinehart & Winston, 1968.

Satir, Virginia. *Conjoint Family Therapy.* Palo Alto, California: Science & Behavior Books, 1967.

Simonton, O. Carl and Stephanie. *Getting Well Again.* Los Angeles: Jeremy P. Tarcher, 1978.

Watzlawick, Paul; Bavelas, Janet Beavin; and Jackson, Don D. *Pragmatics of Human Communication.* New York: W. W. Norton & Co., 1967.

INDEX